THE
EDIBLE
FLOWER

THE EDIBLE FLOWER

A Modern Guide to Growing, Cooking & Eating Edible Flowers

Erin Bunting & Jo Facer

Laurence King Publishing

CONTENTS

INTRODUCTION

One evening in late March 2016 we were having a going-away party in the Skip Garden in King's Cross, London. It was a freezing evening, but it was magical, huddling around the fire pit, drinking beer, eating pizzas from the wood-fired oven in an urban garden rooted in the seasons and the community. We were both secretly hoping we could create a little slice of that magic and ethos in our new lives.

In a couple of days' time we'd vacate our terraced house in east London, pack our two ginger cats into the car and drive to Northern Ireland to start a new life. We had almost no idea what we were doing, but we had a vague notion that we wanted to live in the countryside and start a business that involved cooking and growing food. A lot happened in the six months after we left London. We started a supper club and catering company; our first catering job was cooking all the meals for fifty bluegrass musicians for three days in the dungeon-like basement of a private boarding school. It was a baptism of fire!

Jo started an organic vegetable growing course and volunteered with a local organic market gardener. We hosted half a dozen supper clubs and found an audience for our events. We bought a farmhouse and smallholding in the drumlins (hump-backed hills) of County Down, moved in and promptly turned over the whole lawn to a huge kitchen garden. And we are still here, cooking for others, hosting supper clubs, teaching people to cook, grow and brew beer, making pizza in our own wood-fired pizza oven and growing vegetables, salads and edible flowers for ourselves, our events and to sell to others.

Our business is all about our passion for good food. We make food by hand, from scratch and with love. We serve it with merriment – and often with home-brewed beer. Our business connects us and our clients to the earth (the worms, the planet and the seasons) and we aim to consistently produce delicious, inspiring, surprising and beautiful food. We called ourselves The Edible Flower because for us, growing, cooking with and eating edible flowers summed up the ethos of our business.

It is our aim to share that joy through this book. It is a guide to the edible flowers we grow and cook with most often, the ones we've found to be the tastiest and the most useful, and the ones we can grow easily in a temperate climate. It is not a compendium of all edible flowers everywhere, but instead a helpful guide to help you create your own edible flower garden and then enjoy eating it.

As with many small businesses, we both do a bit of everything, but it's primarily Jo's job to grow produce and Erin's to make it delicious. And that is how we've approached this book – Jo has written the gardening sections and it's Erin's voice in the recipes.

Why Grow and Eat Edible Flowers?

We grow edible flowers primarily because they bring us great joy. They are beautiful in the garden, and beautiful when we use them in food. They bring pollinating insects into our garden in great numbers. We don't get many calories from edible flowers, but we get some unique flavours and a big helping of happiness; there is something truly magical about growing food from scratch and then eating it.

The food we cook at The Edible Flower is rooted in rustic home cooking; flavour, seasonality and stories are important to us, as well as generosity and beauty. Our food isn't fine dining and it definitely isn't about one perfectly placed flower petal in a fancy restaurant. Although Erin is a keen baker – and uses lots of flowers in her bakes, as you will see – we don't primarily think of edible flowers as a pretty garnish for cakes. Fine dining and cake decorating are where people most often encounter edible flowers, but sometimes they can just feel like a decorative add-on. We want to show you that they can bring unique flavour, beauty, seasonality and an opportunity to slow down and literally 'smell the roses'.

Flavour – Many edible flowers have delicious and interesting flavours that you won't encounter anywhere else. Sometimes that flavour is announced by their smell (think of lavender, roses or chamomile), but sometimes it is more surprising. Nasturtiums smell of roses and honey but are full of peppery punch; magnolia's sweet, citrus smell belies its strong, spicy, gingery flavour. Think of using edible flowers for their flavour the way you might use fresh herbs: sprinkle spicy calendula petals over your salad instead of basil; use mild, cooling borage flowers instead of mint; or substitute bright, menthol lavender for rosemary in marinades or when roasting meat or vegetables. As with herbs, spices and other aromatics, you can preserve the flavour of edible flowers by drying them or by making cordials and syrups, floral sugars and vinegars to use all year round.

Beauty – We think flowers are beautiful, so why not use that beauty to make your food look glorious? A handful of edible flower petals tossed through a green salad transforms it from everyday to special, while delicate violas used to top gingerbread biscuits make them into a splendid gift.

Seasonality – We live in rural Northern Ireland, in the northwestern United Kingdom. It is not the most hospitable of climates for growing flowers, so if we can grow something, you probably can too. We have long, dark winters, and at midwinter we have only six or seven good daylight hours. Our edible flowers are seasonal, and we don't currently grow in polytunnels or under heat lamps, although we will overwinter a few flowers in our greenhouses to extend the season a little. For us, cooking with edible flowers is a way of marking the changing of the seasons, of signifying that this food is from this place at this very moment. The delicate violas and primroses of late winter are joined by calendula, borage and tulips in mid-spring. As we tip towards the summer solstice the hedgerows are full of elderflower and hawthorn and the garden has jaunty cornflowers, chamomile, dill and wispy coriander. Once all danger of late frost has passed, we can look forward to the summer bounty of nasturtiums, marigolds, dahlias, courgette (zucchini) flowers and more. As the season winds down, we hope the frosts don't come too soon so that we can enjoy our tender edible flowers late into the year. The icy morning when we find that all the nasturtiums have turned to mush always marks the time to start using the stores of floral treats we have preserved over the kinder months. We hunker down with the fire lit and wait for the cycle to begin again.

Slowness – Growing from scratch, picking and processing edible flowers for cooking and eating isn't the quickest process in the world. It requires thought and care. And this is one of the reasons we love it. We are both doers; we have to-do lists as long as our arms and are always trying to be faster and more efficient. But when you want to harvest or cook with edible flowers, you must slow down. It takes delicacy to harvest them and time to process them; it forces you to relax a little, to lose yourself in the meditative task of plucking the petals from a pile of cornflower heads. It connects you to the earth and the seasons. And serving your guests with a dish containing the thousands of cornflower petals you picked so carefully shows all the love, care and attention you put into preparing that dish for them.

How to use this book

This book is intended to inspire you to eat and grow something new, regardless of your level of gardening and cooking experience. It is divided into two sections. The first is all about how to grow edible flowers in general; the second is a directory of flowers, with specific growing advice and lovely recipes for each.

If you are experienced at growing vegetables, you might want to jump ahead to the directory and start incorporating edible flowers into your growing plans for an increasingly vibrant and pollinator-friendly kitchen garden. Experienced ornamental growers may find you already grow many of the flowers covered in this book, so you can start dipping into our recipes as soon as the season is right.

If you are new to gardening, or find yourself in a new garden, we would encourage you to read some of the general gardening and garden-planning advice before reading about the specific flowers. And if you have no interest in gardening, or no garden, consider purloining some flowers from your neighbours, family or friends to get you cooking!

The recipes in this book are divided by flower, so if you want to find a recipe for borage or roses, for example, go to that particular flower section.

Some key skills, such as pressing and drying edible flowers, making floral sugars, and making syrups and vinegars, apply to many different flowers. How-to sections on these are included under an appropriate flower, with details of how they apply to other flowers, too. Some of the recipes, although attributed to a particular flower, can be made with others, and there are notes on this in the individual recipes. Think of the recipes in this book as a starting point, and start to experiment with your own ideas as you get used to incorporating flowers into your cooking.

Botanical names – Throughout this book we use a combination of common names (e.g. carnation) and Latin or botanical names (e.g. *Dianthus caryophyllus*). Each botanical name is unique, so this is sometimes the only way to ensure you are talking about a specific plant; this is particularly important if you're going to be eating a plant.

Words that appear after the Latin name, as in *Dianthus caryophyllus* 'Giant Chabaud', refer to a particular cultivar (cultivated variety) of that species with particular characteristics, in this case highly scented double blooms.

How to Grow Edible Flowers

The more I grow, the more I delight in the fact that growing can be so simple and effortless. When it works, it feels as though you barely do a thing – the seeds, soil, sun and rain do all the hard work for you. Your plants are lush, healthy, pest-free and of course delicious. It's magical. But when things go wrong, it can feel overwhelming and complicated. It's very easy to get bogged down in specific (sometimes contradictory) advice on exactly how to grow a particular plant or deal with a particular pest. With the unbelievable highs of seeing a seed germinate and grow into something beautiful and delicious come the terrible lows of seedlings getting entirely eaten by slugs overnight.

That is why this section starts with some general growing advice. Concentrate on working with nature to improve your growing environment (primarily the soil), and the plants will look after themselves – more or less.

How we grow

Here at The Edible Flower, we try to grow food (and the very occasional non-edible plant) as simply and sustainably as possible. We use a set of principles and approaches borrowed from a mixture of movements: organic gardening, no-dig gardening, regenerative agriculture, forest gardening, permaculture and agroecology. The common thread running through all these movements is that we aim to work with nature, not against it.

My priority is always to look after the soil. I feed the soil, not the plants, by using organic material to feed soil organisms, in the form of a layer of compost added to the surface of my vegetable and flower beds annually. I recognize and respect the delicate ecosystem of life in the soil and I try to minimize disturbing it.

I try to grow plants well, choosing the right plants for the conditions, getting the timing right and protecting plants when they are young and vulnerable. I grow most of my plants from seed in a greenhouse.

I control pests and diseases naturally, and my aim is to achieve a natural balance between pests and predators. I avoid monocultures (large areas of the same crop), provide habitats for predators and where necessary use my wit and cunning against pests, often in the form of a physical barrier to protect plants at the right moment.

I'm going to try to convince you that if you concentrate on the following key approaches for your garden, growing edible flowers – or anything else – will be simple and pleasurable.

Learn to love your soil – If I could encourage all gardeners to do just one thing, it would be to get to know and learn to love their soil. Soil is complicated, but here I cover the basics that I think any gardener should understand.

Soil is a mixture of mineral particles, organic matter, air and water. It is often classified based on the size of mineral particle that it contains. These particles are called sand (the biggest particle), silt (medium) and clay (the smallest). A soil with a balanced mixture of sand, silt and clay is called a loam. One with a lot of sand is a sandy soil and one with lots of clay a clayey soil. Sandy soils drain well but don't hold on to moisture or nutrients. Clayey soils hold on to nutrients and water, and can even become waterlogged. We have a clayey soil at The Edible Flower.

This classification based on the size of soil particles is called **soil texture**. Generally speaking, when it comes to soil texture, you work with what you've got. There isn't much point in trying to change it. However, regardless of your soil texture, you can always improve your soil in other ways. The best way is to add organic matter, such as compost. This improves the **soil structure** – that is, the way the soil clumps together into crumbs. It improves the drainage of your soil, regardless of texture, and its ability to retain nutrients. It also feeds the microfauna in the soil.

Feed the soil – This is a fundamental principle of organic growing: feed the soil, not the plants. (The non-organic approach is to ignore the soil, instead providing nutrients to the plants using soluble fertilizers, which can

why this is a bad idea for your plants and the planet in the long term).

When I say 'feed the soil', what I'm actually saying is feed the soil organisms: worms, beetles, bugs, fungi and bacteria. There is a whole ecosystem of life in healthy, undisturbed, balanced soil, and if you want to grow great plants easily, enlisting the help of this army of microfauna is crucial. They make nutrients available to plants, and importantly, these are stable insoluble nutrients that can hang out in the soil until the plants need them. Your plants will be healthy, they will grow at sensible rates and they will be far less susceptible to pests and disease.

Another way to put this is that soil biology trumps soil chemistry. Good soil life is more important than the particular chemical make-up of your soil, and if your soil is full of life, you can get away with imperfect soil chemistry.

So, what do soil organisms eat? Well, of course, some eat other soil organisms (soil protozoa eat soil bacteria, for example), but in terms of the food you're going to provide, it is carbon-based materials, or organic matter, primarily in the form of compost. Compost is just a word for broken-down organic matter, whether that be composted kitchen and garden waste, composted horse manure or even composted wood chips.

In a natural ecosystem such as a forest, plants or bits of plants die and fall to the surface of the soil (or lie under the soil, in the case of roots), and the soil organisms eat them from below. It's a balanced cycle of growth and decomposition, with all the nutrients being recycled between plants, soil organisms and the soil.

In your garden, it's a bit different. You take vegetables, fruit or flowers away from your garden to eat them or admire them in vases. You also take away weeds, and plants that have finished being useful. It's your job as the gardener to replace what you take away, and you do this in the form of compost. All plants need, and therefore seek, slightly different combinations and quantities of nutrients from the soil. These nutrients end up in the leaves of the plants, and if the leaves end up in your compost heap, they will create a diverse, balanced diet for your composting microfauna and an array of nutrients in your compost. When you spread that compost over your vegetable and flower beds, that array of nutrients will feed an array of soil organisms and ultimately make growing happy, healthy plants as easy as it can be. That brings us to the next rule.

Mulch, don't dig – To be honest, I was pretty surprised to learn how strong the culture was of digging in vegetable growing and gardening. (When I say digging, I mean using a garden fork to incorporate organic matter into the soil.) It really is a lot of hard work.

No-dig gardening, or no-till farming, an approach that is being adopted more and more around the world both in gardens and on farms, gets rid of this hard work. And, rather than being just as good as the digging approach, it seems as though magic things happen when you stop disturbing the ecosystem and the delicate physical structure that exists just a few inches below the surface of the soil.

Instead of digging, you mulch. You add a layer – say 2.5 cm (1 in) – of compost to the surface of your flower or vegetable beds, or around your trees. This is food for the soil organisms. It is their job to incorporate it slowly over time, as required. But this layer of organic matter does other wonderful things to your soil. It improves the soil's ability to hold on to water, and it also magically improves the drainage . It helps you achieve the horticultural holy grail of soil that is both water-retentive and free-draining.

After you've been mulching and growing in the same place for a few years, you will have glorious soil. If you dig down a little bit (say to plant a dahlia tuber), you will see how the dark, crumbly organic matter is slowing being incorporated into the lower levels of the soil. The soil will be firm enough for your plants' roots to grip, but friable enough that you can whip out any weed seedlings easily.

Get weed-free – Being on top of weeds is a wonderful feeling. It makes you want to hang out in your glorious weed-free garden. Once you're weed-free, it's really quite simple to stay that way. And being weed-free isn't just something to aspire to if you want a neat garden; if you want to grow good flowers, vegetables or anything else, it's a no-brainer. Weeds compete with your plants for light, water and nutrients. They are also hiding places for slugs and other pests. And, most importantly, if you have weeds you have to weed all the time because they will spread, whereas if you don't have weeds it all becomes much easier to manage.

I would advise you to create growing spaces in your garden that are limited in size, based on your willingness to stay on top of the weeds. Grow intensively and weed-free in a small area, rather than having a bigger area with no time to weed it (leave other areas wild and the wildlife will love it). Get on top of the weeding, using light exclusion – see below – or by digging out your weeds, then stay that way through hoeing or hand-weeding.

* **Light exclusion –** All plants get energy from the sun through the amazing process of photosynthesis. If a plant is not photosynthesizing, it's getting weaker, and if it keeps getting weaker it will die. A very simple way to kill weeds is by excluding light. You can do it with any opaque material: a piece of black plastic or thick wool carpet, geotextile or a thick layer of compost. The vast majority of perennial weeds will die after 12 months of this treatment. It may sound like a long time, but plan ahead and you will be delighted with the results.

Mulching your bed with compost each year is a form of light exclusion, since soil is a seed bank for weed seeds. All naturally occurring topsoil will contain lots of dormant seeds that may have been there for years, and if you expose that soil to the light, those seeds will germinate and start to grow. By regularly covering the soil with compost (which should be relatively free of weed seeds) and gardening in a way that avoids disturbing the soil as much as possible, you will never expose the weed seeds to the light, so they will never germinate and won't cause you any problems.

* **Dig it out –** If light exclusion isn't practical and you have some well-established perennial weeds (weeds that survive from year to year,

such as nettles, brambles, buttercups and dandelions), digging them out may be your only option. I use a hori-hori knife to dig out as much of the crown of the plant as possible without disturbing the soil too much. If you don't get all the root out, don't panic, just repeat the process if a new set of leaves appears. The weed will be using up its stored energy (often in the form of starch in its thick roots) in creating new shoots, and as long as you remove the leaves before it can replenish itself from the sun you will exhaust it.

* **Hoeing –** You will always need to do a bit of weeding to stay on top of your weeds. There may be weed seeds in your compost, or seeds may be blown in from elsewhere. A quick hoe to knock the top off very small weed seedlings is all you need, and I recommend an oscillating hoe, or hand weeding for very small beds or high raised beds. The smaller the weed seedlings the better. Above all, you want to avoid a weed going to seed, which would mean you have to do lots of extra weeding weeks or months later. If you're harvesting flowers or other produce, that's the ideal time to pull out any tiny weeds you notice.

Make compost – Making compost is one of the most important things we can do in the garden, because it's food for all the soil organisms. 'Compost' simply means organic matter that has been broken down (i.e. 'eaten') by micro-organisms. Before it is 'ready', the ingredients (leaves, grass clippings, shredded twigs and so on) will still be recognizable. When it is ready to use, it should be uniformly dark brown and crumbly, and should smell clean and earthy.

It's easy to make compost, although it is tricky to do quickly. These are the six key elements for successful home composting:

* **Balance green and brown materials** – 'Green' materials (kitchen peelings, grass clippings, weeds) are rich in nitrogen and generally damp. 'Brown' materials (straw, autumn leaves, twigs, newspaper) are rich in carbon and often quite dry. Layer up a diverse mixture of

the two – humans thrive on a varied diet, and so do compost heaps and soil organisms.

If you find your compost is smelly and waterlogged, mix in additional brown material. If it isn't breaking down and is dry and twiggy, add some green material. Mixing in a load of grass clippings is a really useful boost in this situation, but do make sure the grass doesn't sit in a claggy lump on top.

* **Moisture** – About 70 per cent moisture is optimal. A dried-out compost heap will do nothing for years. Aim for the moisture level of a wrung-out sponge: wet, but not dripping or waterlogged. You can water your heap to make it wetter, or mix in grass clippings. Cover your heap to keep moisture in and avoid it becoming too wet in rainy weather. I find a piece of old carpet laid over the top is ideal.

* **Heat** – This is vital for fast bacterial breakdown and for killing weed seeds, and the way to achieve it is through volume. I've been lucky enough to visit some colossal municipal green waste heaps in the depths of winter, and the heat is immense! At home, the bigger the better, but the minimum is about 1 cu. m (35 cu. ft) if you want it to generate heat for quick composting. My heaps are 1.5 × 1.5 m (5 × 5 ft) in plan and about 80 cm (32 in) tall. (If you manage to get your heap up to around 65°C (150°F) then the majority of weed seeds should be killed. That means less weeding later on.) Small heaps will still create lovely compost; the process just takes longer.

* **Air** – The primary decomposition processes occurring in your compost heap are aerobic – that is to say, they need oxygen. Air will have been trapped in your heap when you built it. The classic way to keep the process going and reintroduce air is to 'turn' the heap, lifting it all with a fork (I find a lightweight pitchfork ideal) from one spot to another. I've spent several years investigating ways to avoid this hard work, but my conclusion is that it is worth turning your compost heap at least once, normally about three months after you start building it. Not only does this speed up the composting process, but also it is an important way of seeing how your compost is progressing, what has and hasn't broken down. It's how to become a better composter.

* **Surface area** – The larger the surface area of the material in your compost heap, the quicker it will break down. Cut large items into smaller pieces, use a shredder, or mow over bigger bits with a lawnmower before adding them to your heap. Don't put in massive clumps of roots; spend time breaking them up with a spade or fork.

* **Time** – If everything is perfect, between three and six months, otherwise a year or maybe two.

* **What to include** –
YES: Vegetable peelings, teabags, prunings from trees and shrubs (chipped, cut up or mowed over), annual and perennial weeds (ideally no seeds), twigs, torn-up newspaper, wood ash, grass clippings, crushed eggshells, coffee grounds, guinea pig/rabbit bedding, chicken poo, soil (in small amounts).

NO: Cat litter, large sticks or logs, big clumps of roots, very prickly things, cooked kitchen waste, too much of anything.

Creating an Edible Flower Garden

The thought of redesigning a garden can be overwhelming. You may even hold out hope that one day you'll have the savings to employ a professional to do a full redesign and landscaping job. That's a perfectly good option, of course, but if you don't have the finances for it, here I will guide you towards transforming your garden gradually into something productive and full of joy.

This section sets out tasks to do over three years to replan and rejuvenate a garden or part of a garden. It's a 'slow', low-cost, sustainable approach. The primary focus is on creating a garden in which to grow edible flowers, but these guidelines can be applied to growing anything you want.

Three things to do in Year 1

1. Make a compost heap – If you don't already have one, make a compost heap for all your vegetable-based kitchen waste and your garden waste. Ideally this should be located in a sheltered spot, on soil rather than on a patio or decking. Given that sunny areas in your garden are brilliant for growing things, or sitting in, I recommend using a shady spot for composting. If you have space, make a double heap, one for new material and another to turn your compost into once the first is full. When picking your location, think about easy access from the kitchen with food waste, and from the garden.

If you have space for only one heap, size it based on how much waste you will have. Ours was about 0.6 × 0.6 × 0.5 m (2 × 2 × 1½ ft) in our small garden in London, with no lawn. Emptying a single heap should be an annual event. In winter, lift your compost bin off the compost (assuming it's small enough to lift), whether it's full or not. Put the newish material from the top of the heap back into the compost bin, and spread all the well-rotted compost sitting below over your vegetable and flower beds.

2. Get to know your site – Observe the sun, and note the shady and sunny spots. If you often experience strong winds in your garden, think about where they come from and where are the sheltered spots. Notice if you have any frost pockets (areas that stay frosty even when the rest of the garden or the rest of the neighbourhood has thawed). Observe waterlogged and very dry areas. Think about existing plants that will compete for water, nutrients and light with plants you want to introduce, and bear in mind that the roots of trees and hedges will extend horizontally as least as much as the height of the plant. Observe the plants that you already have and work out what they are, especially if you like them.

For the most part, simply actively observing what is happening in the garden is enough in your first season. Note down the date of the first and last frost. Record any plants that you like and want to keep, perhaps by taking photos of them throughout the season. And, for herbaceous perennials (plants that die back in winter but come again in spring), it's worth marking their location with a stick in autumn, when you can still see them.

3. Grow your first edible flowers – Rather than trying to squeeze new plants into existing beds in your first year, I recommend finding a good sunny spot, creating a new bed and growing annuals from Chapter 1 for at least one season. You could grow some tall, brilliant-blue cornflowers and borage at the back of the bed, with colourful calendula and nasturtiums in front. Or grow vegetables and herbs for their flowers – courgettes (zucchini), mustard leaves, coriander (cilantro) and dill, interplanted with little clumps of viola.

Growing annuals is a great way to start in a new bed. You get a chance to observe what grows well where, and, with an empty bed at the end of each season, you can make sure the soil is free of weeds. (Don't worry too much about weeds in the rest of the garden yet.)

If you haven't got the time or space to create a whole new bed in your first year, try growing in pots instead. All the flowers in Chapter 1 can be grown in containers.

Create new beds – Each year I make more beds for growing vegetables and flowers. I've learned that maintaining a lawn by simply mowing it regularly in summer is almost as much work as maintaining a vegetable bed, once you've managed to get on top of the weeds. So I regularly turn little awkward corners of grass, or large areas of lawn or pasture, into beds.

There are a few ways to do this, but regardless of your technique, the aim should be to improve the soil through the addition of organic matter, and to reduce weeds, ideally to zero. Here are the techniques I regularly use. You can try this at any time of year, but I generally do it in late winter so the beds are ready for planting in spring.

* Cover with black plastic – This isn't pretty, but it's very effective. Cover the area you want to turn into a bed with black plastic, or something else robust and opaque, for a whole growing season. Remove the plastic in winter or spring, when all the grass or weeds should be dead and you can cover the area in a thin layer of compost (say 2.5 cm/1 in, depending on how rich your soil is) and then start planting. The compost should cover the surface of the soil entirely. Weed seeds (of which there may be many) in the soil will not be exposed to the light, and so won't germinate. If there is something particularly rampant in the area, such as docks or brambles, you can dig out their crowns before covering, or after you take the plastic off if you missed them initially.

* Cover with card and compost – I often use this technique to create a new bed when I haven't managed to think ahead by a whole season. Mow the area so the grass or weeds are short. Cover the area with a double layer of cardboard (not shiny cardboard, the brown stuff, with any tape or staples removed), then cover that with about 15 cm (6 in) of compost. Tread it down, rake the surface gently to level it, then plant straight into the bed. The advantage of this technique is that you can do it all in one day, including planting seedlings if you've got them ready. The disadvantages are that you need plenty of compost, the grass and weeds dying under the rotting cardboard make a great habitat for slugs, and you may need to make temporary sides for your bed (I use lengths of scrap timber) to hold the compost in place during the first year. By your second season of growing in the bed, the cardboard will have rotted away completely and the compost will have started to become incorporated into the soil below.

* Build raised beds – A raised bed should ideally be on soil, rather than an impermeable surface. Not only does the soil beneath provide drainage, but also it provides a connection to soil organisms that you want to encourage into your bed. There is no need to clear the area of weeds or grass before building the bed. Build the edges and then fill it up with soil and compost. Use a layer of card under the soil if you're worried about weeds breaking through, or just use the soil to smother the weeds or grass below.

A raised bed can be very low – just 15 cm (6 in) tall – and created in the same way as the previous technique, but with edges that are permanent rather than temporary. Or your raised bed may be tall, in which case there will be less bending down to harvest your flowers, but you'll need to find lots of soil and compost to fill it. Compost will sink down a lot in the first years, so ideally use soil to fill up most of the bed, and top it with compost. If you need lots of soil, think about digging a pond. As well as being great for minimizing what you bring on to and off the site, ponds are great for wildlife and biodiversity, and digging is great exercise!

* Rejuvenate an old bed – You can follow the advice above on creating a new bed, and build it directly over an old bed. However, you will need to dig out any big plants you don't want. If you're unsure, leave the odd plant in the bed for the first year; you can always dig it out later.

Three things to do in Year 2

1. Learn from your plants.
Understand your microclimates –

You will now have been growing annuals in your first edible flower bed for one season. If you observed that plants did worse in some parts of the bed than in others, try to figure out why. Is there competition for water from a hedge or tree? Did the shaded areas do better because they dried out more slowly in hot weather? Did the lower areas do worse because the ground was waterlogged? Did the strip along a fence do badly becauseof a 'rain shadow', which meant that none of those plants got any water all year?

2. Remove and move plants –

By now you should have a good idea of what plants already exist in your garden, and whether you like them or not. The winter after your first season of growing is a good time to dig out or cut down plants you don't want.

If you like a plant but it is in the wrong place, take cuttings if it's a woody plant, or dig it up if it's a herbaceous perennial. You can divide the latter and grow the plantlets in pots for a season before planting into their new locations the following year.

When removing woody plants, hire or borrow a shredder and put the material in your compost bin or spread it directly on beds as a mulch. Alternatively, cut it up with secateurs or loppers and stack it all in a shady corner of the garden to create an amazing habitat for wildlife. We're lucky to have lots of hedgehogs in our garden, and I take full credit for that fact, because there is a massive pile of woody material that I had set aside for shredding but never got round to!

3. Plant herbaceous perennials and develop more growing spaces –

After a year of observing what is happening in your garden and how you use it, you should be in a good position to write a list of what you want in the garden and where, but by sticking with annuals (which die after each season) and herbaceous perennials (which can easily be lifted and moved) you still have plenty of flexibility in your garden design.

Grow some herbaceous perennials or woody herbs (see Chapter 2) in the weed-free beds you created in the first year. Your first edible flower bed could now be filled with chives, agastache, thyme and lavender in any sunny, well-drained areas, or full of colourful dahlias and perennial tulips (this last is a good combination, because the dahlias hide the unsightly tulip leaves as they die back).

If you want more growing space, create more beds (see page 19) and initially grow some more annuals. Focus on getting your beds free of weeds and with healthy soil full of organic matter and soil life, and plant more permanent perennials in these beds later.

Year 3 and beyond

1. Think about the verticals and plant woody perennials –

Your garden is a complex place. You must think about its two-dimensional, geometric plan and space your plants accordingly. You must also think about how the plants change with the seasons. With luck, after a few years of growing annuals in pots and beds, and planting and moving around herbaceous perennials, you'll have a good sense of what works. Now it's time to think about your vertical space, and where you want permanent height.

As you move away from annuals and start to design the framework of 'permanent' perennials, try to think about the garden in horizontal layers. At the top level, you have the canopy of trees, with a lower level of shrubs below. Below that, you have ground-cover plants, both woody herbs and herbaceous perennials. Within this permanent framework of perennials, you might have large gaps or clearings that create sunny spaces for sitting (lawns, patios) or growing annuals (vegetable patches and flower beds).

Plant trees or shrubs (see Chapter 3), making sure you have a good sense of how big they will grow over time. Choose dwarf cultivars if you have a small space. Planting trees or shrubs into weed-free, healthy soil that you've been growing annual or herbaceous perennials in for several years will give them the best possible start in life.

You can also use fences, screens or pergolas to create height and as structures to support climbing plants.

2. Collect seeds and take cuttings –

Collecting seeds (see page 138) and taking cuttings (see page 294) to create new plants can become addictive. It's a great way to swap your favourite plants and varieties with friends and family and to fill up your garden with the plants you love to grow and to eat.

Your garden will never be finished. But that is surely the joy of gardening. Even if you decide to grow exactly the same annual edible flowers in the same place each year, the weather will change, the cultivars will be different and each year your soil will improve. You will learn to do things slightly differently – perhaps slightly better – and the result will be a new garden each year. Your edible garden could be many things but, most of all, I hope it brings you joy.

Spring Sowings

If you're new to growing edible flowers, this is a great place to start. All the flowers in this chapter are annuals (or perennials that are grown as annuals). You sow seeds and plant out the seedlings, then, after the flowers are over, pull them out and throw them on the compost heap. They are quick and easy to grow. You get to experience the delight of growing something from seed, and if it all goes wrong, you get another try next year.

Annuals are plants that complete their life cycle in a year or less. They germinate from a seed, grow into a plant, produce flowers and seeds, and die, all in one growing season. The term 'hardy' indicates that a plant is able to tolerate freezing temperatures (as opposed to tender plants, which will die if exposed to frost). Hardy plants have different levels of hardiness, depending on how far below 0°C (32°F) they are able to tolerate.

This chapter contains many hardy annuals. Because hardy annuals can survive cold weather, they are typically grown from seed in early spring. They can be planted outside before the last frost, and will flower that summer. (For an earlier harvest, they can even be sown the previous autumn and overwintered in a cold frame or unheated greenhouse, or outside in milder areas.)

This chapter also contains a few tender plants (carnations, courgettes/zucchinis, French marigolds, nasturtiums) that are native to warmer climates. In temperate climates such as that of the UK, Europe and much of the USA, these are often grown as 'half-hardy annuals'. 'Half-hardy' is a confusing term that implies some degree of hardiness, but in fact half-hardy annuals are not hardy at all. They can be sown in spring in a protected environment such as a greenhouse, polytunnel, conservatory or windowsill (not in the ground outside), but warmth may be needed to help the seeds germinate. The seedlings should be planted out only after the last frost.

GROW PLANTS FROM SEED

I sow almost all my annuals in some sort of container in my unheated greenhouse, rather than directly in the ground. This means I get better, healthier seedlings exactly when and where I want them, and the slugs and snails don't get a chance to eat the tiny seedlings just as they pop up.

There are many ways to produce healthy seedlings to plant out. This is how I do it. Rather than using modular trays, seed trays, pots, cardboard egg boxes, coir starter pellets or paper pots, I use soil blocks. I make little compressed cubes of compost using a soil-block maker, and they sit in a seed tray with small gaps between them.

There are a few reasons why I choose to do it this way. First, it's a very flexible system – with just one soil-block maker and some trays of any shape or size I can sow as many seeds as I want. Second, because there are small air gaps between the blocks, when a tiny root grows to the edge of the block and hits the air, rather than going round and round in circles (as it does when it hits the inside of a pot or module) something called 'air pruning' happens. The rootlet stops growing and bushes out inside the soil block. This results in seedlings with really healthy, bushy root systems, which are ready to start growing as soon as you plant them out into the ground.

1.

I use a mixture of organically certified, peat-free seed compost, horticultural sand and water to make my soil blocks, at a ratio of about 3:1:1. The mixture should be quite wet. Mix it all together on a board or work surface and push it into a mound approximately twice the height of the finished soil blocks. Push the soil-block maker down on to the mound and press it firmly against the surface, twisting it from side to side. Water should squeeze out of the top as you make the blocks; if it doesn't, think about adding more water. Use the handle to push the soil blocks out into your tray. See if you can pick one up easily without it breaking up. If it's too fragile, try varying the mix by adding more water or a little less sand.

2.

After making a tray of soil blocks, I put the seed carefully into the indentation at the top of each one. As a general rule, very small seeds should be planted very shallowly, with only a sprinkling of compost over the top, and larger seeds deeper. A depth that is equal to twice the diameter of the seed is a good guide. There is no need to water the soil blocks at this point.

3.

Place the blocks in their tray somewhere light and reasonably protected. This could be a greenhouse, cold frame, windowsill, polytunnel or conservatory. Check the seed packet or have a look online to find the ideal germination temperature for each type of plant. For seeds that need higher temperatures to germinate, a warm windowsill is a good option, or wait until later in the season when the ambient temperature is higher.

The time it takes for a seed to germinate depends on the species and on temperature. In general, seeds germinate and seedlings grow more quickly in warmer temperatures.

4.

Plant out seedlings when they are still quite small – with perhaps three or four 'true' leaves ('true' leaves are those that come after the first pair of leaves, which are known as 'seed' leaves and look pretty much the same on any plant). A good rule of thumb is six weeks from sowing to planting out in the cooler spring months, and four weeks in the height of summer.

5.

You may need to 'harden off' your seedlings before planting them out. In a greenhouse, with warmth and no wind, your seedlings will grow fast but the growth will be soft. If you're planning to plant them out when the weather is cool or the wind is strong, you can toughen them up by putting them in a cold frame for a few days beforehand. Alternatively, plant them out and then cover them in horticultural fleece for a few days or weeks, depending on the weather.

I sow thousands of seeds each year, and my joy when I see each successful germination doesn't diminish. Experiment with different methods, timings, cultivars and species and find what works for you and your garden. Always sow too much, and – despite the name of this chapter – continue to sow throughout the growing season for successional crops. Aim always to have some spare seedlings in case a few plants or even a whole area of plants fail. I hate seeing empty beds, and love seeing them overflowing with vegetables and flowers.

BORAGE

Borago officinalis

Hardy annual

Height up
to 0.8 m (2½ ft)

Spread up
to 0.5 m (1½ ft)

Sun or partial shade,
well-drained soil

Sow in spring

Harvest flowers in
summer and autumn

Why we grow it – Borage plants are big and hairy-leaved with beautiful small, star-shaped blue flowers. They are easy to grow and will self-seed readily. They release a delightful cucumber aroma as you brush past, and are always teeming with bees. Both flowers and leaves are edible, with a distinctive cucumber-like flavour. It's magical to add a couple of flowers to a gin and tonic or a glass of Pimm's, and they make beautiful floral ice cubes.

How to propagate – In early spring, sow seeds individually in modules or soil blocks in a greenhouse or on a windowsill. Borage has large seeds that are easy to handle. I collect them each autumn for sowing the next year (see page 138 on how to collect seed).

Some growers advise sowing borage seeds directly into their final positions, because the plants don't like to have their roots disturbed. However, I've never had any problems with growing them in modules. I've found that you can even carefully dig up self-seeded borage seedlings and transplant them to your chosen location.

How to grow – Borage likes a reasonably sunny spot. When your seedlings are large enough to handle, plant them out about 40 cm (16 in) apart. I grow mine in blocks alongside vegetables, but it would work equally well in flower beds and borders or large containers. At my recommended spacing the plants will get very tall, with their thick, hollow stems growing surprisingly fast. They have a strong tendency to flop over if not supported. Depending on the location, I either prop them up with pea sticks, corral a block of plants together with posts and string, or just let them flop.

How to harvest and prep – Use scissors, or your thumb and fingernail of your first finger pushed together, to cut through the stem just behind the flower. Alternatively, if you find that the hairy leaves and stems of borage irritate your skin, wear gloves and long sleeves and use scissors to harvest.

Store the flowers in a sealed container in the fridge and use within 24 hours. Just before use, you need to 'de-fuzz' your borage – that is, remove the hairy sepals. Use one finger and thumb to hold the stem and sepals, and the finger and thumb of your other hand to hold the flower gently by its anthers (the pointy black bit in the middle of the flower). Gently prise the sepals and stem away from the flower.

FLOWERS *all summer and into autumn.*

DO *eat the flowers (de-fuzzed) raw in salads and cocktails. The young leaves are also edible raw or cooked.*

DON'T *cook or press the flowers. They don't store well.*

TASTES *like cucumber.*

PICKLED KOHLRABI, CUCUMBER & BORAGE SALAD

We make a version of this pickled salad at least once a week in summer. Its cooling sweetness is amazing with curries, while the acidity cuts through the richness of slow-roasted meats and it is delicious loaded into a sandwich or pitta with leftovers the following day. Vibrant blue borage adds colour and a soft cucumber flavour, but this salad also looks amazing with peppery calendula petals. I particularly like shredded aniseedy agastache in this salad, but if you aren't growing agastache, mint is a delicious alternative.

Serves 4

2 tbsp sugar

3 tbsp rice vinegar
or white wine vinegar

3 tbsp water

¼ tsp salt

1 medium kohlrabi

1 medium cucumber

2 shallots

4 radishes

1 or 2 red chillies, or to taste

a handful of agastache or mint leaves

20 borage flowers, defuzzed

1.

Put the sugar, vinegar, water and salt in a small pan over medium heat. Stir until the sugar and salt dissolve, then bring to the boil and simmer for about a minute. Remove from the heat and allow to cool a little.

2.

Meanwhile, peel the kohlrabi. I do this with a potato peeler. Peel it quite vigorously, as beneath the skin there is often a layer of thicker flesh that can be tough to eat. Cut the kohlrabi into matchstick-sized pieces.

3.

Slice the cucumber in half lengthways and then, using a teaspoon, scoop out and discard the seeds. Cut the flesh into slices about ½ cm (¼ in) thick, slicing on an angle for the best look. Peel the shallots, cut in half lengthways and slice into half-moons. Trim the radishes and slice into thin rounds. Deseed the chilli(es) and chop finely. Put the kohlrabi, cucumber, shallots and chilli in a bowl and pour over the cooled dressing.

4.

Chiffonade the agastache or mint by bunching the leaves together, rolling them up into a tight tube and slicing them very finely into long strips. Stir through the salad. Leave for about 30 minutes before eating, or store in the fridge for a few days. Just before serving, defuzz the borage flowers (see page 35) and sprinkle them over the salad.

BORAGE

TUSCAN BEAN STEW WITH BORAGE LEAVES & GREEN PESTO

It would be a shame to miss out on borage's fresh-tasting leaves. Borage traditionally had a reputation for bestowing courage and cheerfulness, and for me, this dish is the epitome of comfort food. It is flavoursome and hearty, but also packed with goodness. It takes a while to prepare, and indeed the longer you cook the base vegetables the better, so it is a good dish to make while you are pottering about in the kitchen. It freezes well, so make a big batch against future melancholic emergencies.

Borage leaves add a cooling freshness to any dish and are a natural thickener for soups and stews. Pick young leaves for eating, as older ones can become very thick and prickly.

Serves 6

2 tbsp olive oil

1 large onion, finely diced

1 large carrot, finely diced

1 fennel bulb, finely diced

1 red chilli, finely chopped (or use ½ tsp chilli flakes)

4 garlic cloves, finely chopped

2 × 400 g (14 oz) cans borlotti beans (you could also use cannellini)

400 g (14 oz) can tomatoes

2 bay leaves

600 ml (20 fl. oz) vegetable or chicken stock (broth) (it's fine to use a stock/bouillon cube)

150 g (5½ oz) kale (or other leafy greens such as chard or savoy cabbage)

100 g (3½ oz) stale bread

100 g (3½ oz) young borage leaves, sliced into thin strips

salt and freshly ground black pepper

To serve, grated Parmesan and a handful of de-fuzzed borage flowers

1.

Heat the oil in a large, heavy pan or casserole dish (Dutch oven) and add the chopped onion, carrot and fennel. Season with 1 tsp salt. Reduce the heat to low, cover and cook for as long as you can – at least 30 minutes, but if I have time I will cook mine for 90 minutes. The longer you cook this base (or soffritto, as the Italians call it), the more sweetness and melding of flavours in the final dish. Stir it occasionally so that it softens but does not brown.

2.

About 10 minutes before you plan to finish cooking the vegetables, add the chilli and garlic to the pan. Stir well and continue to cook. Ten minutes later, add the beans with their liquid, the tomatoes, bay leaves and stock. Add a good grind of pepper and a little more salt if needed. Bring to the boil, then reduce the heat and simmer with the lid on for 30 minutes.

3.

Meanwhile, to make the green pesto, chop the herbs or salad leaves and walnuts in a food processor. With the motor still running, drizzle the olive oil in through the funnel in the top until the mixture forms a thick green paste. Stop the motor, add the lemon juice, ¼ tsp salt and the sugar, and scrape down the sides. Blitz again and then taste, adding more salt, sugar or lemon juice if necessary. If you don't have a food processor, chop everything very finely and stir in the oil and seasoning.

4.

Remove and discard any woody stems from the kale, then slice the leaves into strips about 1 cm (½ in) wide. Break or cut the bread into small pieces, a couple of centimetres (about 1 in) wide.

5.

After the soup has been simmering for 30 minutes, add the borage leaves, kale and bread and cook gently for another 10 minutes or so, until the greens are tender.

6.

Serve hot, garnished with the pesto, grated Parmesan and borage flowers.

For the pesto:

50 g (1¾ oz) soft green herbs and/or peppery salad leaves (such as wild garlic, parsley, coriander/cilantro, mustard leaves, rocket/ arugula, watercress, sorrel)

30 g (1 oz) walnuts

50 ml (2 fl. oz) olive oil

juice of ¼ lemon

a pinch of sugar

CALENDULA OR POT MARIGOLD

Calendula officinalis

Hardy annual

Height and spread up to 0.5 m (1½ ft)

Sun or partial shade

Sow in spring

Harvest flowers in summer and autumn

Why we grow it – If you grow just one edible flower, this should be it. Calendula brings such joy. Its large, bright orange, daisy-like flowers are a glorious pop of colour, and have many uses in the kitchen. It is equally at home in containers, flower beds or vegetable beds, and if you remember to deadhead it will flower all summer. The petals dry really well (see page 86) and can bring colour and cheer to your winter meals, too.

How to propagate – In early spring, sow seeds individually in modules or soil blocks in a greenhouse or on a windowsill. I also sow extra seeds throughout spring and summer to fill up any small gaps in the garden. Calendula seeds are large enough to handle easily.

The seeds are very easy to save to add to your collection for next year. If you are collecting seeds from a mixed patch (calendula is often sold as a mixed collection), tie pieces of coloured wool around the stems of the flowers you like, while they are still flowering. That way you will know which seeds to save when the time comes.

How to grow – I grow calendula everywhere: in my vegetable bed, in our borders and in pots. I always plant several seedlings together to form a block of colour. Plant out your seedlings when they are large enough to handle, spaced about 25 cm (10 in) apart. Keep deadheading throughout summer and they will keep flowering.

Each year, some of my calendula plants suffer from powdery mildew, a fungal disease that appears as a dusty white coating on the leaves. Plants that are water-stressed (thirsty) are particularly susceptible, so remember to keep them watered, particularly those in pots. It can also be helpful to use the no-dig approach, so that the mulch of compost helps to retain moisture in the soil.

How to harvest – Calendula flowers are quick and easy to harvest by hand. Just snap through the stem immediately behind the flower, or leave it longer if you want the flower with its stem for pressing or as a cut flower. The whole flower is edible, but most of the time it's the beautiful petals that you will use in the kitchen. To remove the petals, give the flower head a couple of firm taps on the table and shake to remove any bugs, then, holding the flower by the stem, pluck off the petals a few at a time into a bowl.

FLOWERS *all summer and into autumn.*

DO *eat the petals raw or cooked. Store whole flowers in the fridge or dry the petals. Whole, single-headed flowers also press well, but they must be really dry when you harvest them.*

DON'T *forget to deadhead to keep the flowers coming.*

TASTES *peppery and a little spicy.*

THE EDIBLE FLOWER

RIBBONED COURGETTE & AVOCADO SALAD WITH POPPY SEEDS & CALENDULA

CALENDULA OR POT MARIGOLD

When courgettes (zucchini) are in season, from mid-July until early October, we harvest half a dozen or more every day. It's a frantic race to keep up with the garden! Peppery calendula petals are the perfect foil to the gentle flavour of the courgettes, and the pop of orange against the soft green courgette and avocado is a joy.

**Serves 6
as a side dish**

800 g (2 lb) courgettes (zucchini)

3 tbsp olive oil

1 lemon

1 tbsp poppy seeds

petals from 4 calendula flowers

1 large ripe avocado

Sea salt and freshly ground black pepper

1.

Top and tail the courgettes and slice them into ribbons using a potato peeler. If they are big you might want to set aside the central flesh, which will be a bit watery. You can keep it in the fridge and add to a pasta sauce or soup.

2.

Heat a large frying pan (skillet) over medium heat, then add half the olive oil. When the oil is hot, add half the courgette ribbons and fry for a couple of minutes, until soft. Remove from the heat. Season with salt and pepper, a little lemon zest and a squeeze of lemon juice to taste. Put to one side in a large bowl, then repeat with the other half of the courgette ribbons. When all the courgette is cooked, stir in the poppy seeds and half the calendula petals.

3.

Cut the avocado in half, remove the stone (pit), peel and slice into half rings. Squeeze a little lemon juice over the flesh to stop it from discolouring.

4.

Arrange the courgettes on a flat plate or platter and add the sliced avocado, tucking it in among the courgettes. Sprinkle over the remaining calendula petals. Serve warm or at room temperature.

POT MARIGOLD
SODA BREAD

Soda bread is ubiquitous in Ireland. It is quick to make, and there is no need for proving because the rise is created by the combination of acidic buttermilk and alkaline bicarbonate of soda (baking soda). This focaccia-style loaf with lots of olive oil, rosemary and calendula petals is in no way traditional. The flowers make it a gorgeous centrepiece for the lunch or dinner table.

Makes 1 loaf

4 tbsp olive oil

500 g (1 lb 2 oz) plain (all-purpose) flour

1 tsp bicarbonate of soda (baking soda)

1 tsp salt

2 tsp finely chopped rosemary, needles only

23–28 calendula heads

400 ml (14 fl. oz) buttermilk

sea salt, for sprinkling

1.

Preheat the oven to 200°C/400°F/Gas 6. Line a deep 30 × 20 cm (12 × 8 in) baking tray (pan) with baking parchment and drizzle with 2 tbsp of the olive oil.

2.

Sift the flour and bicarbonate of soda into a large mixing bowl, add the salt and whisk to combine. Stir in the rosemary and the petals from 8 of the calendula flowers. Make a well in the centre and pour in most of the buttermilk. With your hand in an open claw shape, quickly mix the wet and dry ingredients until you have a slightly sticky dough. If it is too dry, add the remaining buttermilk.

3.

Put the dough into the prepared baking tray, then with clean hands gently press the dough out until it completely covers the tray in an even layer. Working quickly, press the remaining whole calendula flowers into the top of the bread.

4.

Drizzle the remaining olive oil over the bread and flowers and spread it out using a pastry brush so that everything is covered in oil. Sprinkle with sea salt and put in the oven. It's important to bake the bread as soon as possible so that you get a good rise from the reaction between the buttermilk and the bicarbonate of soda.

5.

Bake for 15 minutes, then turn the oven down to 180°C/350°F/ Gas 4 and bake for another 25 minutes, until golden. This bread is best eaten fresh, but will be good toasted for another couple of days.

SOUPY WHITE BEANS WITH BROAD BEANS & CALENDULA

Calendula brings joyous flecks of orange and a subtle umami-pepperiness that goes beautifully with the beans in this dish. Be generous with it: twenty heads might seem excessive, but you want lots of those golden flecks. You can also use dried calendula; add 3 tbsp dried petals as you reheat the beans. This makes a brilliant vegan main course, served with bread for dipping, but if you don't need it to be vegan, finely grating Parmesan or another hard cheese on top just before serving is delicious.

The beans in this dish must be soaked overnight before cooking. For a much quicker version, use two or three jars of good-quality cooked cannellini beans. Just add them with their liquid and 1–2 tsp thyme leaves to the cooked celery, onion and wine mixture in step 4 and proceed from there.

Serves 6

For the beans:

500 g (1 lb 2 oz)
dried cannellini beans

small bunch of thyme
(about 6 stalks)

1 stick celery

1 small onion, peeled,
roots trimmed, cut in half

1 small carrot

4 garlic cloves,
unpeeled, lightly crushed

1½ tsp salt

1.

The day before you want to make the dish, put the dried beans in a large bowl and add at least twice the volume of cold water. Leave to soak overnight.

2.

The next day, drain the beans and put them in a large pan. Add fresh water to cover the beans by about 2.5 cm (1 in). You don't want to add too much because this water forms the liquid in the dish. Add the aromatics: thyme, celery, onion, carrot and garlic.

3.

Increase the heat and bring the mixture to the boil, then turn down to medium-low and simmer uncovered for about 45 minutes, stirring occasionally. Skim off and discard any white scum that rises to the surface.

4.

While the beans are cooking, heat the olive oil for the stew in a wide pan over a medium heat. Reduce the heat to low, add the onions, celery and garlic with a generous pinch of salt, and cook for about half an hour, until completely soft but not coloured. Increase the heat to high, immediately add the white wine and allow it to bubble vigorously for 10 minutes, or until the liquid is reduced by about half.

5.

Check the beans every so often to see if they are cooked, and if the pan looks dry add 200 ml (7 fl. oz) more water. How long dried beans take to cook depends on their age. When they are cooked they will be soft, still holding their shape but not chalky when you bite into them. Remove from the heat and fish out the aromatics using a slotted spoon. Add the salt and stir well. The consistency should be like a stew, not as runny as soup. If it is too loose, scoop out a bit of the liquid; if it is too thick, add a little boiling water.

6.

Add the onion, garlic and celery mixture to the beans and stir well.

7.

Bring a small pan of water to the boil, throw in the broad beans and cook for 2 minutes, no more, then drain immediately and refresh in cold water. Slip off the pale skins to reveal their vibrant green loveliness.

8.

To make the gremolata, mix the parsley and garlic and stir in the lemon zest.

9.

Reheat the beans, then taste and season with more salt and pepper if necessary. Just before serving, stir in the broad beans, calendula petals and lemon juice to taste.

10.

Serve in warmed bowls with a sprinkling of gremolata on top.

For the stew:

4 tbsp olive oil

2 onions (about 300 g/10 oz in total), finely chopped

4 sticks celery, finely chopped

2 garlic cloves, finely sliced

250 ml (8½ fl. oz) white wine

1 kg (2¼ lb) broad (fava) beans, podded

petals from 20 calendula flowers, fresh or dried

juice of half a lemon

salt and freshly ground black pepper

For the gremolata:

20 g (½ oz) flat-leaf parsley, finely chopped

1 garlic clove, finely chopped

finely grated zest of half a lemon

CARNATION

Dianthus caryophyllus

Short-lived evergreen perennial, often grown as a half-hardy annual

Height up to 0.7 m (2¼ ft)

Spread up to 0.4 m (1¼ ft)

Sun or partial shade, well-drained soil

Sow in spring

Harvest flowers in summer and autumn

Why we grow it – The intensity of taste varies across the various species and cultivars, but as a general rule dianthus petals taste of cloves, with hints of nutmeg or black pepper. We primarily grow *Dianthus caryophyllus*, the traditional, scented, tall-stemmed cut flower, for the kitchen, because it has excellent flavour. The world of carnations (also known as dianthus or pinks) is a taxonomically confusing place, and there are also *D. barbatus* (sweet william), *D. alpinus* (alpine pink), *D. chinensis* (China pink), *D. deltoides* (maiden pink) and others; all are edible.

How to propagate – We sow carnation seeds in early spring, keeping them in the greenhouse for several weeks until the last frost has passed and it's safe to plant them out. They are rather slow to get established but should give you a great supply of flowers in late summer and autumn.

If you live in a frost-free location they can be grown as a perennial. Confusingly, some cultivars of *D. caryophyllus* are hardy and will survive the winter, particularly if your soil is well drained. If you are growing carnations as perennials, it is worth noting that they are short-lived perennials and so will decrease and die after a few years, so take softwood cuttings in early summer (before they flower) to renew your stock of plants.

How to grow – Carnations are tall and wispy, and have a tendency to flop over if they are not supported. We mainly use willow domes, but for a large patch of carnations, netting or wire mesh supported about 30 cm (12 in) above the ground is ideal.

Chickens and rabbits love eating the leaves, but other than that, carnations have few problems with pests or disease. Stormy weather and heavy summer rain can damage the plants and flowers, so if you have a large greenhouse or polytunnel, carnations are definitely a candidate for growing in a protected environment.

How to harvest – Pick whole flowers with or without stems. They will last well after harvesting in the fridge or in a vase with water. Buds will continue to open after harvesting. Keep picking the flowers to keep them coming.

FLOWERS *from late summer into autumn.*

DO *use the flowers in syrups, cordials and infusions.*

DON'T *forget to deadhead.*

TASTES *sweetly spicy, of cloves.*

FLORAL BABKA WITH CORNFLOWERS & CARNATIONS

CARNATION

This is an enriched bread filled with lots of my favourite things: pistachios, cardamom, orange zest, and lots and lots of flowers. Do see the recipe as a blueprint, and experiment with other sweet-scented edible flowers. I've made a version with rose sugar and rose petals, for example. Don't scrimp on the flower petals. It seems a lot for one loaf, but you need to see all the colours when you cut into it. Dianthus syrup adds flavour and a glossy pink glaze.

Makes 1 loaf

For the cornflower sugar:

150 g (5½ oz) caster (superfine) sugar

4 heaped tbsp dried cornflower petals or 10 tbsp fresh (I like to use pink or red cornflowers for the sugar)

For the filling:

75 g (2¾ oz) whole shelled pistachios

100 g (3½ oz) butter, cubed

100 g (3½ oz) white chocolate, chopped

1 tbsp milk (if necessary)

5 cardamom pods, crushed, husks removed, ground to a fine powder

zest of a small orange or half a large one

30 cornflowers

25 small dianthus flowers or 10 larger carnations

1.

Preheat the oven to 180°C/350°F/Gas 4. While it is heating, put the caster (superfine) sugar and cornflowers in a food processor or a scrupulously clean spice or coffee grinder and blitz to combine. If you don't have an electric grinder, you can use a mortar and pestle, but it will take a while.

2.

Now make the filling. Spread the pistachios out on a baking tray (pan) and toast for 5 minutes in the oven. Allow to cool, then chop roughly and set aside. Turn off the oven.

3.

Grease a 900 g (2 lb) loaf tin (pan) and line bottom and sides with baking parchment. Leave a little parchment overhanging on the long sides to help you take the cooked loaf out of the tin.

4.

Over a very low heat, stir together the butter, 125 g (4½ oz) cornflower sugar and the white chocolate in a small pan until melted and combined into a smooth sauce. If it splits a little, don't worry; add 1 tbsp milk, stir vigorously and it will return to a smooth sauce. Add the ground cardamom and orange zest, then set it aside to cool and thicken while you make the dough.

For the dough:

300 g (10½ oz) plain (all-purpose) flour

½ tsp salt

1 tsp (5 g/⅛ oz) fast-action dried yeast

zest of a small orange or half a large one

5 cardamom pods, crushed, husks removed, ground to a fine powder

2 eggs, lightly beaten

100 ml (3½ fl. oz) whole (full-cream) milk

75 g (2¾ oz) butter, at room temperature, cubed

For the syrup:

either 200 ml (7 fl. oz) dianthus syrup (see page 66) or

75 g (2¾ oz) sugar and 35 ml (1 fl. oz) water

5.

Put the flour in the bowl of a stand mixer with the dough hook fitted. Add the salt, yeast and remaining cornflower sugar, being careful that the yeast and salt don't touch. Add the orange zest, ground cardamom, eggs and milk and mix on the low setting for 2 minutes, until a rough dough has formed. Turn the machine up to medium and add the butter cube by cube, making sure the first cube is fully incorporated before you add the next. Once all the butter is added, continue to knead for 5 minutes until it is smooth, glossy and not too sticky.

You can knead the dough by hand, but it will take quite a bit longer. Try to knead it somewhere cool on a cold surface, otherwise the heat of your hands may cause the butter to melt and run out. If the dough starts to feel warm, put it in the fridge for 15 minutes to firm up.

6.

Lightly flour a work surface and roll the dough out into a rectangle approximately 30 × 40 cm (12 × 16 in), with the long side facing you. Spread the cooled white chocolate mixture all over the dough, leaving a space of 1 cm (⅜ in) around the edge. Sprinkle over the chopped pistachios and then the flower petals. Roll up the dough from the long side (closest to you) into a tight Swiss roll, ending with the seam tucked underneath. You will now have a rolled-up sausage of dough 40 cm (16 in) long. Cut a little off each end to neaten.

7.

Rotate the doughy sausage 90 degrees so that one short side is facing you. Using a sharp knife, cut vertically down the middle of the dough, so that you have two long pieces of dough with

the filling showing. Place the far end of one piece on top of the other and push together gently to seal. Then, without stretching the dough, make a simple two-strand plait (braid) or twist by lifting one piece of dough over the other. Keep plaiting until the dough runs out, then secure the two ends by pushing them together. Tuck both ends of the dough underneath to form a loaf that is about the length of your loaf tin. Gently lift the babka into the tin, then cover (I seal mine into a really large freezer bag) and leave somewhere warm to rise for 1½–2 hours. The loaf should just come up to the top of the tin, but not overflow.

8.

About 15 minutes before you want to bake the loaf, preheat the oven to 200°C/400°F/Gas 6. Bake for 15 minutes, then turn the oven down to 180°C/350°F/Gas 4 and bake for another 25 minutes, or until a skewer inserted into the middle comes out clean.

9.

While the loaf is baking, make the syrup. If you are using dianthus syrup, put it in a small pan, bring to the boil and bubble vigorously for about 5 minutes, until reduced by about half. Alternatively, put the sugar and water in a small pan over a low heat and stir to dissolve the sugar. Once dissolved, increase the heat to medium and bring to the boil and simmer for one minute then remove from the heat.

10.

As soon as the loaf comes out of the oven, brush the syrup all over it – it will soak in best when the loaf is warm. Allow the loaf to cool before removing it from the tin. It will keep for a couple of days in an airtight container, but is best eaten fresh.

CARNATION & BLACKBERRY COOLER

I find that you can extract the flavour from even not particularly scented carnation by making a syrup. The petals also give up their colour in the boiling water, so if you use coloured flowers you end up with a beautiful pink or red syrup that looks and tastes amazing in a cocktail. I often use frozen blackberries, since they cool the cocktail as you make it. It works well without the vodka, too, but you might want to add a splash more syrup to taste.

Rose syrup (see page 66) also works really well in this drink.

Serves 2

For the carnation syrup (makes about 400 ml/13 fl. oz):

15 g (½ oz) carnation petals (about 30–40 flowers)

300 g (10½ oz) sugar

For the cocktail:

50 g (1¾ oz) fresh or frozen blackberries

a few basil leaves, plus extra to garnish

100 ml (3½ fl. oz) vodka (optional)

juice of 1 lime

300 ml (10 fl. oz) sparkling water

a couple of carnation flowers, to garnish

1.

To make the syrup, put the petals in a bowl or jug (pitcher), pour over 300 ml (10 fl. oz) boiling water and leave to infuse (steep) overnight, or for at least 12 hours.

2.

Strain the resulting liquid into a small pan and add the sugar. Heat gently, stirring, until the sugar has dissolved, then increase the heat and simmer for a minute. Remove from the heat and allow to cool, then pour the syrup into a bottle or jar and store in the fridge. It should last for a couple of weeks in this way; for longer storage, I recommend freezing it.

3.

To make the cocktail, put the blackberries and basil in a cocktail shaker or jug (pitcher) and crush together with a cocktail 'muddler' or the end of a wooden spoon. Add 80 ml (2¾ fl. oz) dianthus syrup, the vodka and lime juice, and shake or stir well.

4.

Put ice cubes in two highball glasses and strain half the mixture into each glass. My cocktail shaker has a coarse strainer that means some, but not all, of the blackberry bits end up in the drink. If you like, you can use a sieve (strainer) to strain the mixture and then add a little of the crushed blackberries back to the drink. Top up with sparkling water and garnish with basil and carnation flowers or petals.

MAKE FLORAL SYRUPS & CORDIALS

There is no definitive difference between cordial and syrup, and I use the terms interchangeably in this book. Cordial, perhaps, implies that it will be diluted and served as a drink, and syrup implies a wider use: for poaching fruit, drizzling on cakes, adding to dressings or flavouring ice creams. Both are made with sugar, water and flavourings – in this case edible flowers.

There are a few different ways to extract the flavour from flowers for syrup, but the primary difference is when you add the sugar. My preferred method is to add the sugar at the end of the process, once the flowers are strained out, and I haven't yet found a scented flower for which this doesn't work.

1.

To make a syrup, put your chosen flowers or petals in a heatproof container. As a rule, I find removing as much of the green parts or stalks as possible results in a prettier coloured syrup and with a less bitter taste. Pour boiling water over the flowers and leave to infuse (steep) for several hours, usually overnight. The ideal quantity of flowers to water varies depending on flower and flavour; there is a guide for some of my favourites on page 66, but do experiment to find what suits you.

2.

Taste the mixture a few times, and strain the flowers out when the flavour is strong enough. If you are looking for a stronger flavour, you can strain the flowers out, bring the liquid back to the boil, pour it over a fresh batch of flowers and leave to infuse again overnight. The resulting liquid might taste a little bitter, but that should be balanced out when you add the sugar.

3.

Once you are happy with the flavour, strain the liquid through a piece of muslin (cheesecloth) or a clean dish towel, to remove any bugs or pollen, into a measuring jug (pitcher). Make a note of the amount of liquid you have. Pour it into a pan and add an equal quantity by weight of granulated sugar – if you have 250 ml (9 fl. oz) liquid, for example, add 250 g (9 oz) sugar. Stir over a medium-low heat until the sugar dissolves, then turn up the heat and simmer for about a minute before removing from the heat and allowing to cool. Pour into bottles and store in the fridge for a couple of weeks, or keep in the freezer.

For a thinner syrup, use less sugar, and for a heavier syrup you can add more. Thicker syrup is great for drizzling over ice cream, and can always be thinned with water.

* **Carnation/dianthus syrup –** 15 g (½ oz) petals to 300 ml (10 fl. oz) water (see recipe on page 62)

* **Rose syrup –** 15 g (½ oz) petals to 300 ml (10 fl. oz) water (see recipe on page 23)

* **Magnolia syrup –** 20 g (¾ oz) petals to 300 ml (10 fl. oz) liquid. This makes a delicious gingery, cardamom-scented syrup perfect for use in a Moscow mule or over a sticky pudding

* **Violet syrup –** If you can find scented violets (*Viola odorata*), the scent will be very strong, but even less scented violets will yield a Parma violet flavour. Using 10 g (¼ oz) violets (or more if you have them) to 300 ml (10 fl. oz) water will yield a beautiful deep purply-blue syrup that will turn pink when you add acid (such as lemon juice). Use to make Aviation cocktails

* **Elderflower syrup –** 6–8 large heads of elderflower and 1 lemon (zest in long strips and juice) to 300ml (10 fl. oz) water. Remove all the leaves and as much stem as possible. See also recipe for Elderflower and Lime Syrup Cake on page 253

* **Lilac syrup –** 30 g (1 oz) flowers to 300 ml (10 fl. oz) water

* **Hawthorn syrup –** 30 g (1 oz) flowers to 300 ml (10 fl. oz) water

* **Sweet geranium syrup –** 4 large leaves, chopped, to 300 ml (10 fl. oz) water. In fact, I most often just add a leaf or two of sweet geranium to another cordial; it goes particularly well with rose and German chamomile

* **German chamomile syrup –** 10 g (¼ oz) flower heads to 300 ml (10 fl. oz) water

* **Lavender syrup –** 2 tsp flowers to 300 ml (10 fl. oz) water

CORIANDER/ CILANTRO

Coriandrum sativum

& DILL

Anethum graveolens

Hardy annuals

Height up
to 1 m (3 ft)

Spread up
to 0.3 m (1 ft)

Sun or partial shade

Sow in early spring or
late summer and autumn

Harvest flowers
in midsummer

Why we grow them – In the kitchen garden, both coriander and dill will send up tall stems topped with gorgeous flower heads in midsummer, followed by seeds. We eat the leaves, flowers and seeds, and use coriander root in curry pastes. Coriander and dill are not related, but they are grouped here because I grow them in exactly the same way.

How to propagate – I sow dill and coriander seeds in seed trays, then prick out the seedlings into module trays once they are large enough to handle. If you sow too much, you can eat the excess seedlings as microgreens. Once they have a few pairs of leaves, plant them out about 20 cm (8 in) apart.

Regardless of when you sow them, coriander and dill will know what time of year it is (they 'sense' whether the day is lengthening or getting shorter), and will always flower around midsummer. If you sow them (as many people do) in late spring, they will almost immediately flower without producing many leaves. This gives many people the impression that dill and coriander are hard to grow. However, if you sow them in early spring you will get a good harvest of leaves before the flowers come. And if you sow them in late summer, they should produce lots of leaves and (if they survive the winter) flower the following year after plenty of new, leafy growth in spring.

How to grow – I grow both coriander and dill in my vegetable patch, but they work equally well in a flower border or in pots.

Once the plants are established, I pick the larger, lower leaves for use as herbs. In summer, once they go to seed and start to shoot up, you can pick the flower heads off as they start to form, for a few extra days of leaf production. However, I generally embrace this new stage of growth and enjoy the flowers instead.

Both plants are hardy annuals, but coriander is slightly hardier than dill. Both survive a mild winter here in Northern Ireland (with just a few nights below 0°C/32°F), but both will die if unprotected outside in a normal winter (some nights down to −5 or −10°C/14–23°F). I cover my earliest spring sowings with horticultural fleece for a few weeks for slightly faster and better-quality early leafy growth. However, I don't bother covering any overwintering plants. I just hope for a mild winter and harvest as required until a really cold spell kills them off.

If you want to save seeds for the following year, remember to wait and collect them from plants that have given plenty of leafy growth before going to seed.

How to harvest – Pick the lower leaves by hand before the plants bolt (produce seed). Later, harvest whole flower heads or seed heads with secateurs or scissors.

FLOWERS *in midsummer.*

DO *eat the leaves, flowers and seeds.*

DON'T *pull the plants up as soon as they start to flower.*

TASTE *strongly of dill and mildly of coriander, respectively.*

THE EDIBLE FLOWER

MEXICAN PICKLED CARROTS WITH CORIANDER FLOWERS

In Mexico, spicy pickled carrots are often served in small dishes alongside evening drinks. They are the perfect foil to a cold beer on a warm evening, and have the great advantage of stopping me from eating quite so many tortilla chips with salsa before dinner. This is our interpretation, using coriander flowers or, better yet, a mixture of coriander flowers and the fresh, aromatic green seeds that form just after the flowers drop their petals.

Makes 1 litre (1¾ pints)

750 g (1 lb 10 oz) carrots, peeled

2 tsp cumin seeds

10 black peppercorns

100 ml (3½ fl. oz) cider vinegar

200 ml (7 fl. oz) jar pickled jalapeños in vinegar

200 ml (7 fl. oz) water

4 garlic cloves, finely sliced

1 tbsp sunflower oil

4 bay leaves

1 tbsp salt

1 tbsp sugar

1 small onion, peeled, cut in half and thinly sliced

20 sprigs coriander flowers or fresh coriander seed heads

1.

Slice the carrots on the diagonal into rounds about 0.5 cm (¼ in) thick.

2.

In a large pan over a medium heat, dry-fry the cumin seeds and peppercorns for about a minute, just until you can smell the spices. Add the cider vinegar, vinegar from the jar of jalapeños, water, sliced garlic, sunflower oil, bay leaves, salt and sugar. Bring to the boil and add the carrots and onion. Bring back to the boil, then lower the heat and simmer uncovered for 10 minutes. Just before the end of that time, add the jalapeños and cook for another minute.

3.

Allow the mixture to cool before spooning into a clean jar or jars, layering with the coriander flowers or fresh seeds until everything is used up. Refrigerate for at least half a day before eating; it is best after a day or two and will keep well in the fridge for a month.

DUCK, ORANGE
& DILL
FLOWER SALAD

Dill flowers are flavour bombs, packed with the fresh, aniseedy flavour of dill but with an added heady, aromatic note that you can feel in your nose. Used sparingly they add lots of flavour and beauty to salads, but they must be balanced out with other strong flavours. Here they contrast deliciously with the savoury duck and sharp, fruity orange.

**Serves 4
as an appetizer
or side dish**

2 duck breast fillets or 1 large duck breast, cut in half

2 oranges

1 large fennel bulb

20 g (¾ oz) whole shelled pistachios

1 dill flower head

sea salt and freshly ground black pepper

a handful of mint leaves, to garnish

For the dressing:

2 tbsp orange juice (saved from the segmenting; see step 2)

2 tbsp olive oil

2 tsp white wine vinegar

juice of half a lime

1.

Season the duck breasts well with salt and pepper, score the skin, and place them skin side down in a cold, heavy frying pan (skillet) or griddle pan. (Starting the duck off in a cold pan, rather than preheating it, ensures that you render out some of the fat, and results in a crispy skin.) Cook over a medium heat for 15 minutes, until the skin is crisp. Turn the duck breasts over and cook to your liking, probably another 5–7 minutes for medium.

2.

Meanwhile, prepare the rest of the ingredients. Segment the oranges by slicing off the top and bottom of the unpeeled fruit, setting them on a flat surface and carefully cutting off the rest of the peel using a sharp knife, aiming to remove all the membrane but leaving as much of the flesh as possible. Then cut the segments away from the central membrane; do this over a bowl, to reserve the juice for the dressing. You should end up with juicy orange segments and no membrane. If the segments are very large, slice them in half to make them thinner, but keep the nice segment shape.

3.

Put all the ingredients for the dressing in a jar, tighten the lid and shake well until combined. Taste to check the seasoning; it should be quite sharp.

4.

Slice the fennel bulbs very thinly using a mandolin or sharp knife. Immediately toss the slices in 1 tbsp dressing and an extra pinch of sea salt to stop them from discolouring.

5.

Roast the pistachios in a dry pan for a couple of minutes or in a moderate oven (180°C/350°F/Gas 4) for 5 minutes. Chop roughly.

6.

Once the duck breasts are cooked, leave to cool and then slice thinly.

7.

To assemble the salad, arrange the fennel on four individual plates or one large sharing platter. Arrange the sliced duck and segmented orange over the fennel and drizzle over the dressing. Break the dill flower head into florets by taking individual flower heads off the long, radial stems. Tuck them among the duck and oranges, and finish by sprinkling over the chopped pistachios and mint leaves.

DILL FLOWER AQUAVIT

Aquavit is a spirit from Scandinavia and northern Europe that is often infused with the anise flavours of dill and caraway. Infusing dill flowers into alcohol is a great way to extract their flavour, and they look ethereally beautiful suspended in the liquid. Taste as you go to avoid the flavour becoming too strong, and strain out the aromatics when the flavour suits you; leaving them in for too long can result in a bitter flavour. In Scandinavia aquavit is generally served neat and very cold as an aperitif or with a meal, but it also makes a great addition to a savoury cocktail such as a martini.

1.

Put the flower heads and lemon zest in a 1 litre (1¾ pint) mason jar.

2.

Pour over the vodka and close the jar. Leave in a cool, dark place to infuse (steep), tasting every few days until you are happy with the flavour. I usually leave it about a week.

3.

Once the flavour is to your liking, strain the vodka to remove the aromatics, and put it in a bottle. Serve chilled straight from the freezer or use as a mixer in savoury and sour cocktails, garnishing with little sprigs of dill flowers for extra gorgeousness.

Makes 1 litre (1¾ pints)

2 dill flower heads, or a few more if they are small

a couple of strips of lemon zest

1 litre (1¾ pints) vodka

CORNFLOWER

Centaurea cyanus

Hardy annual

Height up
to 1.2 m (4 ft)

Spread up
to 0.3 m (1 ft)

Full sun

Sow in spring

Harvest flowers
in summer and autumn

Why we grow it – The vibrant blue of cornflower petals is hard to beat. We grow this British and Irish native – once common in cornfields – for its magical colour, but it is a really hardworking plant. It is beautiful in the garden, great as a cut flower and excellent for pressing whole, and the petals are lovely used fresh in salads, grains and puddings, or dried for use all winter.

How to propagate – Many people (and seed packets) will tell you to sow cornflowers directly into the soil. However, we have had little luck with this method, because slugs or snails eat the tiny seedlings before we even spot them. We sow seeds individually in modules or soil blocks in early spring in a greenhouse or on a windowsill, planting them out once they are established. They are hardy, so there is no need to wait for the last frost.

If you want earlier cornflowers than all your friends, you can also sow seed in autumn to overwinter as seedlings, either directly in the ground or in pots. They will flower a few weeks earlier than spring-sown plants.

How to grow – When planting out, space the seedlings generously about 25 cm (10 in) apart. Unless you get a dwarf variety (such as 'Polka Dot Mix'), cornflowers can become very tall, and to stop them from flopping on to their neighbours you will need to provide some sort of support. We place home-made willow domes (about 55 cm/22 in diameter and 70 cm/28 in

tall) over clusters of three cornflower plants. We also have a large patch of cornflowers where we use large sheets of thick wire mesh supported about 60 cm (24 in) above ground level on sticks pushed into the soil. It's rather flimsy in spring, but as soon as the cornflowers start to grow through it, it becomes self-supporting and very effective.

The main maintenance task is deadheading to keep them flowering. Start picking as soon as they flower, and keep going as long as you can. Collect seed heads in late summer and autumn for sowing the following year.

How to harvest – Snip the flowers off with scissors, leaving the stems long for cut flowers or for pressing. To remove the petals, give the flower heads a shake to remove any bugs, then, holding the flower by the stem, pluck off the petals a few at a time into a bowl.

FLOWERS *through summer and into autumn.*

DO *eat the petals raw or cooked. Store whole flowers in the fridge or pluck the petals and dry them (see page 86). Whole flowers also press well, although the blue colour isn't always preserved.*

DON'T *forget to deadhead to keep the flowers coming all season.*

TASTES *mildly spicy.*

RICE WITH LEMON VERBENA, CARDAMOM & EDIBLE FLOWER PETALS

Lemon verbena is a magical tender perennial that we grow in pots in the garden (and in the greenhouse over winter). It tastes of lemon sherbet, and we often use it in curries instead of lemongrass; it also makes an excellent tea. Like citrus zest, it is wonderful with rice. Serve this dish with a curry or barbecued meat; just make sure it gets its own serving dish, as it looks dreamy with all the petals on top.

Serves 4–6

400 g (14 oz) basmati rice

12 cardamom pods, lightly crushed to open the pods

3 sprigs lemon verbena (or a stick of lemongrass, lightly crushed)

550 ml (19 fl. oz) water

50 g (1¾ oz) butter, cubed

50 g (1¾ oz) sultanas, soaked in hot water for a couple of minutes with a pinch of sugar

a couple of handfuls fresh or dried cornflower and calendula petals

salt and white pepper

1.

Wash the rice under cold running water, until the water runs clear. Drain well and put in a large pan. Add 1 tsp salt, the cardamom, lemon verbena and measured water and bring to the boil, uncovered. Once boiling, put on a tight-fitting lid (you don't want the steam to escape) and reduce the heat to very low. Cook for 15 minutes. Remove from the heat and leave to steam, covered, for another 5 minutes.

2.

When you uncover the rice it should be cooked and fluffy, and all the water will have been absorbed. Stir in the butter, which will melt with the heat of the rice, and the sultanas. Taste and season with more salt, if necessary, and white pepper.

3.

Mix in most of the edible flower petals, reserving a few for the garnish, and heap the rice into a serving dish. Sprinkle over the remaining petals just before serving, and remember to warn your guests about the whole cardamom pods!

You can also make this dish in a rice cooker. Follow the steps above, including the aromatics in your rice cooker.

THE EDIBLE FLOWER

CHOCOLATE MENDIANTS WITH DRIED PETALS

These are really easy and make brilliant homemade gifts or petit fours. Mendiants were traditionally made in France at Christmas, topped with fruit and nuts representing the robes worn by the four mendicant orders – raisins for Augustinians, hazelnuts for Carmelites, dried fig for Franciscans and almonds for the Dominicans – hence the name. I have not limited myself to this colour palette, and have instead used everything in my cupboards.

When melting chocolate it is really important that the chocolate doesn't overheat, or it might split. If you are using a bain-marie, allow the chocolate to start to melt, then give it a stir to help it along. If the water is getting too hot, turn it off and the remaining heat in the water should melt the chocolate. If you are using a microwave, take the chocolate out every 15 seconds and stir it. Once the chocolate is mostly melted, don't put it back in the microwave, just continue to stir and the residual heat will finish the melting process.

Makes about 50 chocolates

100 g (3½ oz) white chocolate

100 g (3½ oz) milk chocolate

100 g (3½ oz) dark chocolate

a selection of toasted nuts and seeds, such as roasted hazelnuts, pecans, pistachios (the green is particularly lovely), pumpkin seeds and sesame seeds, roughly chopped if large

a selection of dried fruit, such as dried cranberries, golden sultanas and dried figs, roughly chopped if large

a selection of dried flower petals, such as cornflower, rose, gorse and calendula

1.

Melt the white chocolate either in a bowl over a pan of barely simmering water (a bain-marie), making sure the water doesn't touch the bottom of the bowl, or in the microwave.

2.

Line a baking sheet with a silicone baking mat or baking parchment. Use a small spoon to put dollops of the melted chocolate on to the lined tray. I find a pointed teaspoon works well – if you pour the chocolate off the point of the spoon where you want the middle of the chocolate to be, it should spread out into a neatish circle 3–4 cm (1½ in) across.

Make about 5 chocolates, then decorate with a mix of toasted nuts, seeds, dried fruit and dried flower petals. Then repeat. Don't dollop all the chocolates out before decorating, or the chocolate will set before you put the toppings on and they won't stick. If the chocolate becomes too thick in the bowl, put it back on the bain-marie for a couple of minutes or in the microwave for 15 seconds to melt again.

3.

Once you have finished with the white chocolate, repeat with the milk chocolate and then the dark chocolate.
Leave to set, then store the chocolates in an airtight container.

DRY FLOWERS

We dry flowers when they are in season so that we can use them for flavour and decoration during the rest of the year. They have many uses: making floral sugars, decorating cakes, flavouring desserts, savoury dishes and drinks, and more. There are a number of different ways to dry edible flowers:

* **In a dehydrator –** This is how I dry most of our flowers, and it is a good choice if you already have a food dehydrator or are planning to dry a lot of flowers.

Spread out the petals or flower heads on the racks (the more spread out they are the quicker they will dry), then turn on the dehydrator. I dry flower petals at 45°C/110°F (almost the lowest setting). They take several hours, but the time varies a lot depending on how full the dehydrator is, how thick the petals are, if you are drying whole heads or individual petals, and if the petals were completely dry when they went in. Check the flowers every few hours. Once they are dry and crisp, put them into completely dry glass jars or other airtight containers while they are still a bit warm.

* **In a low oven –** Spread out the flowers or petals on a baking sheet lined with baking parchment, and put them in the oven at the lowest setting, usually about 50°C/120°F. If your oven has a very strong fan, you might want to turn it off if you can, otherwise the petals will blow about. Check the flowers every half-hour or so, and once they are dry and crisp put them into completely dry glass jars or other airtight containers while they are still a bit warm.

* **Air-drying –** I use this method to dry lavender for use throughout the year; I find that other flowers tend to fade if I dry them this way. Pick lavender with the stems on, tie into bunches with string and hang upside down in a dry place. After a couple of days, as they dry out, I put a paper bag over the flower heads to catch any escapees.

When dry, either pull the flowers off the spikes as and when you need to use them in the kitchen, or pull them all off and store in jars in a cool, dry place.

Flowers that dry well – Cornflower petals, calendula petals, rose petals, carnation petals, German chamomile flowers, chive flowers, wild garlic flowers, gorse flowers, French marigold petals, lavender.

Storing dried flowers – Store them somewhere dark, dry and not too warm. It's crucial to avoid any moisture getting into the jars, or the flowers will go mouldy. If the flowers are kept dry they will last for several years, although the fragrance is strongest during the first year.

COURGETTE/ ZUCCHINI

Cucurbita pepo

Tender annual

Height up
to 0.5 m (1½ ft)

Spread up
to 1 m (3 ft)

Full sun, well-drained soil

Sow in late spring

Harvest flowers in
summer and autumn

Why we grow it – This is one of my favourite plants to grow. It gives an abundance of flowers and fruit from late summer into autumn, and even just one plant may provide more courgettes than you can eat. Eating the flowers (and the tiny courgettes attached to the female flowers) is one way to stay ahead of a glut. However, the more you pick, the more new flowers and fruit will appear, so the glut always comes eventually!

How to propagate – Courgettes are heat-lovers and tender, so we wait until the weather warms in late spring before sowing seed. Sow the large seeds about 4 cm (1½ in) deep in small pots (say 7 cm/3 in), then pot on into larger pots (12 cm/4–5 in) a few weeks later. Harden off the plants and plant out in early summer.

Courgettes are thirsty plants, so, to make watering easier later in summer, when you are planting them out bury the empty pot in the ground next to each young plant. When the weather is dry, just fill the pot with water to ensure the roots get the water they need.

How to grow – Courgettes need lots of space, and I give each plant 1 sq. m (11 sq. ft). You can grow them in large pots, but, as with anything in a pot, they will dry out more quickly than in the ground. They are pollinated by insects, so if you want fruit as well as flowers, they may struggle in an enclosed polytunnel.

Powdery mildew is a very common problem for courgettes late in the season. It can be reduced by watering regularly in dry spells to prevent water stress. My courgettes suffer from it every year towards the end of summer, and I just ignore it and continue to harvest.

How to harvest – Harvest courgette flowers with a knife (and long sleeves – the leaves and stems are scratchy), cutting through the flower stalk. Harvest either male flowers, or female flowers with the small courgette attached. Mid-morning is an ideal time to do it, since the flowers will open some time in the morning depending on the weather. If you are harvesting very early or late in the day, be careful – there may be pollinating insects trapped inside the flowers.

You can use the flowers of winter squash (pumpkins) in exactly the same way as courgette (zucchini) flowers.

FLOWERS *from late summer into autumn.*

DO *harvest with a knife. Breaking flowers or fruit off by hand is just too tricky, and you'll do damage.*

DON'T *forget to pick regularly. Courgettes will rapidly become massive and far less tasty if you forget to harvest for a few days.*

TASTES *of courgette: sweet, fragrant, summery.*

THE EDIBLE FLOWER

COURGETTE FLOWER TACOS

This recipe is inspired by the heaps of beautiful courgette (zucchini) flowers we saw in Mexican markets. Courgettes, squash and their flowers are a core ingredient of Mexican cuisine, and here I've stuffed the flowers with mozzarella seasoned with extra salt to imitate queso Oaxaca, which is what would be used in Mexico. If you can find queso Oaxaca, use that instead. There are quite a few ingredients and elements to this recipe, but don't be put off. The salsa, cabbage and crema just involve chopping and assembly, and can be prepared in advance. The fried courgette flowers will stay crisp in a warm oven for about 20 minutes.

I usually make my own corn tortillas. It is very easy to do if you can find masa harina (nixtamalized corn) – just follow the instructions on the packet. If you don't want to make them, corn tortillas are increasingly widely available, or use flour tortillas instead.

Serves 4

For the pineapple salsa:

half a small pineapple

1 scotch bonnet or habanero chilli (or to taste), finely chopped

1 shallot or ¼ red onion, finely chopped

juice of half a lime

For the cabbage:

200 g (7 oz) red cabbage

½ tsp cumin

juice of half a lime

For the crema:

200 g (7 oz) sour cream

2 tbsp mayonnaise

2 tbsp chipotle in adobo, very finely chopped

juice of half a lime

For the batter:

100 g (3½ oz) plain (all-purpose) flour

100 g (3½ oz) cornflour (cornstarch)

200–220 ml (7–8 fl. oz) cold sparkling water or lager

12 courgette (zucchini) flowers

200 g (7 oz) mozzarella

sunflower oil, for deep-frying

12 corn tortillas (12–13 cm/5 in diameter)

salt

24 sprigs of coriander (cilantro), to garnish

1.

Start by preparing all the fillings. To make the salsa, cut the skin off the pineapple, remove the eyes and the tough core, chop the flesh finely and put in a bowl. Add the chilli and shallot, a pinch of salt and the lime juice and mix well. Taste, and add more salt or lime juice as needed.

2.

Finely slice the cabbage and add the cumin, lime juice and a pinch of salt. Mix really well, to allow the salt and lime to soften the cabbage. I use my hands to give it a good mix and squeeze.

3.

For the crema, mix together the sour cream and mayonnaise. Add the chipotle and lime juice, then season with salt to taste.

4.

To make the batter, mix the flours and ½ tsp salt in a large bowl. Add most of the sparkling water or beer and whisk to mix. Add a little more water if necessary; the batter should be slightly thicker than double (heavy) cream.

5.

Shake the courgette flowers gently to remove any insects and dirt. Divide the mozzarella into 12 pieces and season with salt. Stuff each flower with a piece of mozzarella and gently twist the end of the petals together to hold the mozzarella inside.

6.

Preheat the oven to 100°C/220°F/Gas ¼ and line an ovenproof platter or baking sheet with paper towels. Put sunflower oil in a wok or deep pan to a depth of about 10 cm (4 in) and heat to 190°C/375°F. If you don't have a cooking thermometer, drop a small spoonful of the batter into the oil, and if it bubbles up and browns in 10 seconds the oil is ready. Dip a courgette flower into the batter until it is completely covered, being careful to keep the end twisted to hold in the cheese, and gently drop it into the hot oil. Repeat with three more flowers. (Don't try to cook all the flowers at once, or the temperature of the oil will drop and the batter will go soggy rather than crisp.) Fry for about 3 minutes, turning the flowers in the hot oil until they are crisp and cooked on all sides. They may spit a little if the moisture in the cheese escapes into the oil, so be careful.

7.

Remove the flowers with a slotted spoon, lay them on the platter or baking sheet and put them in the oven to keep warm. Repeat with the next two batches of courgette flowers.

8.

Warm the tortillas, either by passing them over a gas flame using tongs for a couple of seconds on each side, or by putting them into a hot, dry frying pan (skillet) for about 15 seconds on each side. Wrap them in a dish towel to keep warm.

9.

To assemble, put a generous teaspoon of the crema on a corn tortilla. Add the sliced cabbage and pineapple salsa on top and then a fried courgette flower and a couple of sprigs of coriander. Serve immediately.

COURGETTE FLOWER & ROASTED GARLIC TART

This is a great dish if you have only a couple of courgette (zucchini) plants. The flowers look elegant draped over the cream cheese, and you can fill in the gaps with courgette slices. Courgettes taste amazing with olive oil, so don't scrimp when frying them; salt them after cooking, so they don't release too much water and you get that gorgeous golden finish. This tart will stay crisp for several hours, so you can prepare it ahead and serve it later the same day.

Serves 6

1 small garlic bulb

olive oil, for drizzling and frying

1 sheet all-butter puff pastry (320 g/13 oz)

300 g (10½ oz) courgettes (zucchini) (small ones are ideal, and use a mix of different colours if possible), sliced into rounds about 1 cm (½ in) thick

at least 6 courgette flowers, cut in half lengthways

180 g (6 oz) cream cheese

100 g (3½ oz) crème fraîche

2 spring onions (scallions), finely chopped

25 g (1 oz) basil leaves, roughly chopped

a couple of pinches of Aleppo chilli flakes, or another mild chilli flake

sea salt and freshly ground black pepper

petals from 3 or 4 nasturtium flowers, to garnish

1.

Preheat the oven to 200°C/400°F/Gas 6. While the oven is preheating, cut the top off the garlic bulb and drizzle with a little olive oil and a pinch of salt. Wrap the bulb in kitchen foil and put it in the oven.

2.

Unroll the puff pastry and roll it out gently with a rolling pin until it measures about 25 × 35 cm (10 × 14 in). Lay it on a baking sheet lined with baking parchment (you can use the piece that comes with the pastry) or a silicone sheet.

3.

Using a small, sharp knife, and without cutting right through, score a line all the way around the pastry, about 2 cm (1 in) in from the edge. Then scallop the edge of the pastry by using the back of the knife to make deep indents at 2 cm (1 in) intervals all the way around the edge. Finally, use a fork to prick all over the pastry inside the scored rectangle. This will stop the pastry in the middle from rising too much.

4.

Put the pastry in the oven (with the garlic) and bake for 20–25 minutes, until golden brown. Take the pastry and garlic out of the oven and leave to cool.

5.

Heat 1 tbsp olive oil in a wide frying pan (skillet) and fry the courgette slices in batches for a couple of minutes, until golden brown, then turn them over and fry for a minute more. Add a little more olive oil when you need it. Remove the fried courgettes to a bowl as you finish each batch, and season with salt.

6.

Fry the courgette flowers in the same pan, in a little more olive oil, for about a minute, until they are slightly wilted.

7.

Put the cream cheese and crème fraîche in a bowl, and add the spring onions and basil. Squeeze the roasted garlic out of the bulb and add this too. Add the chilli flakes, season with salt and pepper, and mix well.

8.

Spread the cream cheese mixture all over the cooked puff pastry base, keeping it inside the scored line. Drape the courgette flowers over the cream cheese and arrange the courgettes on top. To finish, garnish with nasturtium petals, then slice and serve.

COURGETTE FLOWERS STUFFED WITH BULGAR WHEAT, GREEN OLIVES & APRICOTS

Serves 4

6 tbsp olive oil

2 onions, peeled, cut in half and thinly sliced

250 g (9 oz) uncooked bulgar wheat

10 green olives, sliced

50 g (1¾ oz) dried apricots, coarsely chopped

2 tsp ras el hanout spice mix (see page 236)

400 g (14 oz) can chickpeas, drained

juice of 1 lemon

25–30 courgette (zucchini) flowers (depending on size), pistils and stamens removed

300 g (10½ oz) courgettes (zucchini), cut into 1 cm (½ in) slices

salt and freshly ground black pepper

20 g (¾ oz) toasted flaked (slivered) almonds (optional), 2 tbsp Greek (strained plain) yoghurt and ½ tsp sumac, to garnish

This recipe is inspired by a beautiful courgette (zucchini) flower recipe in Georgina Hayden's book of Cypriot recipes, *Taverna* (2019). It's a wonderful way to showcase the flower's delicate flavour. I've given it a Moroccan twist with green olives, apricots and ras el hanout. If you don't have enough flowers at once, supplement with cabbage or large chard leaves. Blanch them in a pan of boiling water for 2 minutes and remove the tough midrib before filling and rolling.

I use the ras el hanout spice mix that we make with dried rose petals and lavender for the Spiced Chicken B'stilla Triangles (see page 236) to flavour the filling. If you don't want to make the spice mix, instead add 1 tsp cumin, ½ tsp each cinnamon and ginger, and plenty of freshly ground black pepper. It will still be delicious.

1.

Heat 1 tbsp of the olive oil in a wide pan over a medium heat, and add the onions with a generous pinch of salt. Reduce the heat slightly and cook for about 4–5 minutes, until the onions are soft and have started to brown and caramelize. If they aren't browning much, turn up the heat for the last couple of minutes.

2.

Put the bulgar wheat in a large bowl and add the olives, apricots, ras el hanout, chickpeas, half the lemon juice, ½ tsp salt, 2 tbsp olive oil and the caramelized onions. Mix well.

3.

Line the bottom of a wide, lidded frying pan (skillet) with the courgette slices. Drizzle with 2 tbsp olive oil and the remaining lemon juice and season with salt and pepper.

4.

Carefully fill each courgette flower with the bulgar wheat mixture. Some flowers will be larger than others, so allocate the filling accordingly. Gently twist the ends of the petals together to seal

the floral packages and place them in the pan on top of the courgette slices, tucking any overhanging petal tips underneath to secure them.

5.

Drizzle over the remaining 1 tbsp olive oil, turn on the heat to medium and add 500 ml (18 fl. oz) boiling water (it should come part of the way up the flowers). Put a large plate face down on top of the flowers to keep them from moving and unravelling. If the plate is a tight fit, put a folded strip of kitchen foil or baking parchment underneath it to help you lift it off later, then put the pan lid on. Simmer for 25–35 minutes, until the bulgar wheat is completely cooked. If there is still a little water in the pan at this stage, remove the lid and cook for a few minutes more to evaporate it; if all the water is gone and the bulgar is still a bit hard, add a splash more water, put the lid on and cook for another 5 minutes.

6.

Allow to cool a little before serving – it is best served warm rather than piping hot. Sprinkle with the toasted almonds (if using) and sumac before serving and add a dollop of Greek (strained plain) yoghurt on the side.

FRENCH MARIGOLD

Tagetes patula

Half-hardy annual

Height and spread up
to 0.3 m (1 ft)

Full sun

Sow in spring

Harvest flowers
in summer and autumn

Why we grow it – French marigolds are a classic 'companion' plant. They are widely reported to reduce aphids and whitefly in tomatoes, because the marigold's fragrant leaves act as an insect repellent, and although I can't verify their effectiveness, I have got into the habit of growing the two together.

How to propagate – In late spring, sow seeds individually in modules or soil blocks in a greenhouse or on a windowsill. French marigolds will be killed by frost if you plant them outside too early, so be patient or grow them in a greenhouse.

How to grow – In the greenhouse, we grow French marigolds around the base of tomato plants and on their own in pots. This means that by late summer, when our tomatoes are in full flow, we also have plenty of gorgeous marigolds. Outside, we grow them in pots to cheer up the courtyard,

and in clumps dotted about the vegetable patch. We have found that deadheading is the only maintenance required.

How to harvest – Pick off flowers and leaves by hand. If the stems are a little tough to break, a knife or pair of scissors will help. The flowers are very long-lasting as cut flowers but also survive particularly well out of water, so are great for decorating cakes, adorning table settings or even wearing in your hair.

FLOWERS *in summer and autumn.*

DO *use the fresh flowers to decorate cakes.*

DON'T *forget that the leaves are incredibly fragrant and edible, too.*

TASTES *citrusy with a good bit of bitterness.*

FRENCH MARIGOLD

MARIGOLD PETAL PASTA

I love the scent of French marigolds, but I'm not a big fan of eating the petals raw, because the citrusy flavour is overwhelmed by bitterness. But I have discovered that once they are encased in pasta and cooked, their herbal flavour with its hint of grapefruit shines through and is a delicious match for a sage butter sauce. I recommend using a pasta machine for this recipe. If you don't have one, ask around – someone may be willing to lend one. You can roll the pasta by hand, but it's hard work and you do need even pieces to fold on top of each other.

All sorts of edible flowers and leaves will work for this recipe, including borage, calendula and nasturtium. Just remember to pick off the petals and use small sprigs of leaves; anything too chunky might tear the pasta.

Serves 4
as an appetizer
or 2 as a generous
main dish

200 g (7 oz) 00 pasta flour (or use strong white flour), plus extra for dusting

2 large eggs

petals from 8 French marigold flowers

a handful of marigold leaves

40 g (1½ oz) butter

20 sage leaves

salt and freshly ground black pepper

grated Parmesan, to serve

1.

Put the flour in a large bowl, make a well in the middle and crack in the eggs. Using a fork, gently mix the flour into the eggs, then use your hands to bring the mixture together into a dough. It might seem a bit dry at first, but it will come together as you knead it.

2.

Turn the dough out onto a clean work surface and knead for about 5 minutes, until the dough is smooth and feels silky. If it still seems dry at this point, knead in a few drops of water. Put the dough in an airtight box or wrap it in cling film (plastic wrap) and leave to rest for at least 30 minutes or up to 2 hours.

3.

Cut the dough in half, dust it lightly with flour and roll it through the widest setting on the pasta machine. Fold the rolled dough like a letter, then pass it through the widest setting again. Repeat the fold and roll through one more time.

4.

Narrow the setting on the pasta machine by one and roll the pasta through again. Keep rolling and narrowing the setting until the pasta is one setting thinner than you want it to be. I roll mine to 6 on my machine. If the sheets become unwieldy, cut them in half. Dust your work surface with flour to stop the pasta from sticking.

5.

Cut the pasta in half horizontally using a pasta wheel, pizza cutter or sharp knife. You should now have two pasta sheets approximately the same size. On one sheet arrange the marigold petals and leaves in a pattern. Then, dusting off any excess flour, place the second sheet on top and press it down gently so that the two sheets are stuck together with the petals and leaves in the middle. If necessary, use a rolling pin to roll over the pasta lightly and stick everything together.

6.

Set the pasta machine to one setting wider than the last setting you used (this is 5 on my machine) and roll the double sheet of pasta through again. Cut the pasta into strips 2–3 cm (1 in) wide. Put the cut pasta on a tray dusted liberally with semolina, or hang it over a pole or clean clothes airer if you are worried about it sticking. Repeat with any remaining pasta sheets, if you cut the pasta earlier because it was getting too large. Then repeat with the second piece of dough.

7.

To cook the pasta, fill a large pan with water and bring to the boil. Meanwhile, put a wide pan over a medium-high heat. When it is hot, add the butter and cook for a couple of minutes, until you start to see brown specks. Immediately toss in the sage leaves and cook for 30 seconds, until the sage is crisp. Remove from the heat.

8.

Once the pasta water is boiling, salt it generously – I use about 3 tsp. Add the pasta and cook for 4 minutes. Drain well and add to the sage butter in the wide pan. Toss the pasta in the butter and season generously with black pepper. Serve in warm bowls, topped with grated Parmesan.

MUSTARDS

Brassica rapa

& ROCKET/ ARUGALA

Eruca vesicaria
Diplotaxis tenuifolia

Hardy annuals

Height up
to 1 m (3 ft)

Spread up
to 0.3 m (1 ft)

Sun or partial shade

Sow in spring or in late
summer and autumn

Harvest leaves
in early summer or in
autumn and winter

Why we grow them – Mustard and rocket are quick-growing, unfussy plants with spicy leaves in a range of flavours, shapes and colours. They can sense the time of year based on the length of the day, and will inevitably start to produce flowers in midsummer. Don't pull them all out immediately; enjoy the flowers in the garden (pollinating insects will love them, including a parasitic wasp that is a very useful natural control for the cabbage white butterfly) and then savour the flowers in your food.

How to propagate – Sowing seed in early spring will give you a good harvest of leaves before the summer flowers. Sowing in late summer or autumn will give you leaves all autumn, into winter and perhaps also the following spring before flowering that summer.

I sow a small pinch of seeds (four or five seeds) in modules or soil blocks. After a few weeks in the greenhouse I plant the seedlings out in clumps at a spacing of 25 cm (10 in). I don't bother to thin out the seedlings, even

if all the seeds have germinated. You can also sow direct in drills or broadcast seed over a large area in early spring.

How to grow – Grow mustard in the ground or in pots. A closer spacing (or smaller pots) will result in smaller, shorter plants with smaller leaves. It's easy to collect mustard seed – see page 138.

How to harvest – Harvest leaves individually by hand or cut back a whole clump of leaves with scissors. Harvest flowers by hand.

FLOWERS *in mid- to late summer.*

DO *use individual flowers raw or pick whole heads of young flower shoots to throw into a stir-fry.*

DON'T *let them go to seed if you don't want many thousands of plants in the same area the following year.*

TASTES *mildly peppery; not as strong as the leaves.*

THE EDIBLE FLOWER

UKRAINIAN
PICNIC CANAPES

This is in no way an authentic dish. I simply wanted to capture the essence of the amazing picnics we ate on a culinary tour in Ukraine with Nataliya Cummings, who runs the cultural exchange Experience Ukraine, and the brilliant cook Olia Hercules. We'd stop for juicy cucumbers, fragrant herbs and delicious homemade soft cheese, with crusty bread and sharp pickles. Back home, we hosted a supper club inspired by the amazing recipes we'd learned. These canapes are light before a big meal and take little time to make once you've pickled the radishes (do this at least 4 hours beforehand). Prepare everything in advance and assemble just before serving.

Makes 30 canapes

For the pickled radishes:

2 tsp sugar

50 ml (2 fl. oz) boiling water

50 ml (2 fl. oz) rice vinegar or white wine vinegar

8 radishes (rounder ones are best), cut into small wedges

For the canapes:

15 g (½ oz) dill

15 g (½ oz) purple or green basil

200 g (7 oz) curd cheese or good-quality cream cheese

zest of half a lemon

80 mustard/brassica flowers

1 cucumber

salt and freshly ground black pepper

1.

Start by making the pickle. Put the sugar and ½ tsp salt in a heatproof bowl and pour over the boiling water, stirring to dissolve. Add the rice vinegar and radishes. Allow to cool, then refrigerate for at least 4 hours, or overnight for maximum pinkness.

2.

Finely chop most of the dill and all of the basil and add it to the cheese with the lemon zest, black pepper and a pinch of salt. Mix well and add more seasoning if necessary. Pick the petals off 50 of the mustard/brassica flowers (reserving the rest for the garnish), add them to the cream cheese and mix again.

3.

If you want to make the cucumber a bit fancier, use a zester to peel thin strips off the skin to give a stripy effect, but this isn't essential. Cut the cucumber into rounds about 5 mm (¼ in) thick.

4.

Arrange the cucumber slices on a serving board or plate, adding the tiniest pinch of salt to each slice. Dollop a small spoonful of the cheese mixture on top of each cucumber round and add a wedge of pickled radish, a tiny sprig of dill and a mustard flower. Serve immediately.

GRAND SALLET

Historically, the grand sallet was the centrepiece of a vast banquet to show off the host's wealth and the estate's abundance. We eat varied green salads all year round, using whatever is best and most abundant in the garden at the time and inevitably brightened with edible flowers. In winter and early spring we eat peppery, bitter salads with lots of chicory, mustard and rocket (arugula), supplemented with young wild greens. In summer and autumn the salads are sweeter, with lettuce and herbs. Think of this recipe as inspiration to celebrate the changing seasons and add unusual ingredients to your salads.

If you are foraging for wild leaves or flowers to include in your salad, please check and double-check that you have correctly identified them as edible. There are many useful books and reputable online resources to help you identify wild ingredients.

Aim to include a wide selection of edible leaves and flowers from your garden. Use your judgement about whether they are tender or sweet enough to be eaten raw. For example, kale, chard, beetroot (beet), primrose, borage and dandelion leaves should all be quite young if they are to be used in a salad.

**Serves 6
as a side dish**

150 g (5½ oz) salad ingredients (see page 116 for suggested incredients)

For the dressing:

80 ml (3 fl. oz) extra-virgin olive oil

40 ml (1½ fl. oz) white wine vinegar

½ tsp soft brown sugar

1 garlic clove, crushed to a fine paste

1 tsp Dijon mustard

sea salt and freshly ground black pepper

1.

Put all the dressing ingredients in a jar, tighten the lid and shake well to emulsify.

2.

Put most of the salad ingredients in a large bowl, reserving some of the more delicate petals and leaves for the garnish. Just before serving, add a couple of tablespoons of dressing and toss well until the salad is just glistening. Taste and add more salt and pepper if necessary. Sprinkle the remaining flowers on top.

Leaves

Red Russian kale
Pentland brig kale
Chard
Sea beet
Beetroot (beet)
Primrose
Viola
Dandelion
Borage
Sorrel
Salad burnet
Marvel of four
  seasons lettuce
Bronze arrow lettuce
Maureen lettuce
Deronda lettuce
Red frills mustard
Giant red mustard
Green frills
  (or golden frills) mustard
Pizzo mustard

Red lion mustard
Wild rocket
Salad rocket
  (arugula)
Mibuna
Mizuna
Spinach
Land cress
Yarrow
Red orache
Fat hen
Pea shoots
Mint
Parsley
Coriander
  (cilantro)
Dill
Chives
Wild garlic
Three-cornered leek
Chicory

Flowers

Borage
Calendula
Mustard
Honesty
Wild rocket
Salad rocket (arugula)
Other brassicas, such as kale
Wild garlic
Viola
Violet
Primrose

Dandelion
Daisy
Tulip petals
Coriander (cilantro)
Cornflower
  petals
Carnation
Chive
Dahlia petals
Nasturtium
Gorse

NASTURTIUM

Tropaeolum majus

Tender annual

Height and spread up
to 0.3 m (1 ft)

Full sun

Sow in spring

Harvest flowers in
summer and autumn

Why we grow it – Nasturtiums are beautiful and very easy to grow, as long as you understand that they do not tolerate frost. I used to suck the sweet nectar out of them in my granny's garden when I was very little, but it must have been three decades later that I ate my first whole nasturtium flower. It's delightfully peppery, as are the leaves. However, I find the fresh green seeds the most surprising. I won't tell you what to expect – just find one and give it a try.

How to propagate – In late spring, sow the large, easy-to-handle seeds individually in modules or soil blocks in a greenhouse or on a windowsill. Nasturtiums are not hardy, and will be killed by frost if you plant them out too soon.

You can collect the seeds easily; just pull them off the plant when green or collect from the ground once they've fallen off the plant, and dry them out thoroughly on a windowsill before storing them in an airtight container somewhere cool for the winter. Nasturtiums will readily self-seed, and if you want them in the same place each year, you may never need to sow them again. However, seedlings won't necessarily be the same as their parent in terms of flower colour.

How to grow – It always feels as though nasturtiums are slow to get going, but then, all of a sudden, in late summer they will be everywhere. Some cultivars are bushy, while others trail or climb, and the trailing ones certainly travel at speed across the vegetable patch if we let them.

Nasturtiums are very easy-going, other than their love of warmth. In poor soil they will produce loads of flowers and fewer leaves. In rich soil, you'll have lots of leaves (including some really big ones) initially, followed by a profusion of flowers later in the season. They are boisterous and joyful in the garden, right up to the first frost – when the whole plant turns to dark green mush overnight.

How to harvest – Pick off flowers, leaves or seeds by hand. To remove the petals, hold the flower by the stem (or the place where the stem would be) and gently detach the petals from the sepal (the yellowy bit behind the petals, that holds them together). Three of the petals are almost round, with a thin stem attaching them to the centre of the flower; they are quite easy to remove. The other two are teardrop-shaped and a bit trickier to remove. Make sure you are holding each one close to the base as you detach it, to ensure it doesn't rip.

FLOWERS *from late summer to late autumn.*

DO *eat the flowers, leaves and seeds.*

DON'T *plant out too early. Nasturtiums are not frost tolerant.*

TASTES *really punchy and peppery; the leaves and seeds are stronger than the flowers.*

ROASTED BEETROOT & TOMATOES WITH YOGHURT & NASTURTIUM SALSA

I love this combination of warm roasted vegetables with cool yoghurt and a drizzle of peppery salsa verde. I particularly love the colours, as the pink beetroot (beet) bleeds into the yoghurt and contrasts with the red tomatoes, the green salsa and the bright orange petals. Use small beetroot if you can – they are generally sweeter. Remember to start making this dish in good time, since it will take you a couple of hours to strain the yoghurt. To save time, you could use Greek (strained plain) yoghurt instead.

**Serves 4
as a side dish**

500 g (1 lb 2 oz) plain yoghurt

olive oil

400 g (14 oz) beetroot (beet)

200 g (7 oz) cherry tomatoes

25 g (1 oz) walnuts

100 g (3½ oz) mixed nasturtium leaves and flowers

10 g (¼ oz) fresh ginger, peeled and grated or finely chopped

a pinch of sugar

1 garlic clove, peeled and grated

salt and freshly ground black pepper

tiny nasturtium leaves or petals, to garnish

bread, to serve

1.

If you are straining the yoghurt, put it in a sieve (strainer) or colander lined with a piece of muslin (cheesecloth) or a clean dish towel and set it over a bowl. If you can, tie up the ends of the cloth and suspend it from a hook or the handle of a kitchen cupboard above the bowl, so that gravity helps to strain the yoghurt more quickly. Otherwise, just give the cloth a little shake or stir every so often to encourage the straining process. Leave it for a couple of hours. You will be left with thin milky-coloured water in the bowl and thick yoghurt in the cloth. You can discard the milky water or keep it to use in bread-making.

2.

Preheat the oven to 160°C/320°F/Gas 3. Scrub the beetroot well and put them in an ovenproof dish with a lid. Drizzle over a little olive oil and season well with salt. Toss the beetroot in the oil and salt until they are well coated, then put on the lid.

3.

Cut the cherry tomatoes in half vertically. Toss with 2 tsp olive oil and plenty of salt and pepper, then arrange on a baking sheet with the cut sides up.

4.

Bake the tomatoes for 1½ hours, until soft, sticky and sweet.
At the same time, cook the beetroot for about an hour, checking
after 45 minutes to see if they are soft by sticking a small, sharp
knife into the centre of one.

5.

Meanwhile, put the walnuts on a baking sheet and roast in the
oven for 15 minutes. Allow to cool and then roughly chop into
large chunks.

6.

When the beetroot are soft, take them out of the oven and leave
them to cool in the dish with the lid on. Sealing the moisture in
means they will be easier to peel once cool.

7.

Once the beetroot are cool enough to handle, peel them and
cut them into wedges. If they are fresh enough, I find the skins
just slip off.

8.

Put the nasturtium leaves and flowers in a food processor with
the ginger and pulse a couple of times until finely chopped.
Drizzle in 4 tbsp olive oil, the sugar and a pinch of salt, and
pulse again briefly to combine. Taste, and add more salt if
necessary. Alternatively, chop everything finely by hand and
mix in a small bowl.

9.

Add the garlic to the yoghurt and season well with salt and
pepper. Put the yoghurt on a plate or small platter, using a
spatula or the back of a spoon to spread it out. Drizzle over two
thirds of the nasturtium and ginger salsa, swirling it a little into
the yoghurt, then arrange the beetroot and tomatoes on top. Dot
over the remaining salsa, sprinkle with the walnuts and garnish
with nasturtium petals or small leaves. Serve with plenty of bread
to mop up the yoghurt.

NASTURTIUM & COURGETTE FRITTERS

NASTURTIUM

Vegetable fritters, pancakes and rostis are essential cooking in our house. They are a brilliant way to use up gluts from the garden or slightly sad vegetables at the bottom of the larder. This recipe is somewhere between a fritter and a pancake and uses buckwheat flour, which is naturally gluten-free. If you want the recipe to be entirely gluten-free, use just buckwheat flour; the flavour will be a little stronger. The nasturtium leaves and flowers add a peppery flavour that is great with lime, and the colourful flecks from the flowers are a pretty surprise as you cut into the fritters.

I like to serve these with a dollop of sour cream, smoked salmon, pickled nasturtium 'capers' (see page 127) and a squeeze of lime juice. They are also great with garlic yoghurt (grate one small garlic clove and add it to 200 ml/7 fl. oz plain yoghurt, with salt and pepper to taste) and chilli oil. You could add a fried egg if you are feeling decadent.

**Serves 4
(makes 10–12 fritters)**

500 g (1 lb 2 oz) courgettes (zucchini)

75 g (2¾ oz) buckwheat flour

75 g (2¾ oz) plain (all-purpose) flour

2 tsp baking powder

zest of 1 lime

a generous pinch of mild chilli flakes (I use Aleppo)

10 g (¼ oz) nasturtium leaves

100 g (3½ oz) fresh peas or frozen peas, defrosted

1 large egg

150 ml (5 fl. oz) milk

75 g (2¾ oz) feta

petals from 30 nasturtium flowers, plus a few extra flowers to garnish

40 g (1½ oz) butter, melted

oil, for frying

salt and freshly ground black pepper

1.

Top and tail the courgettes (zucchini) and then, using the rough side of a box grater, grate them into a bowl. Add ½ tsp salt. Mix well and leave for 15 minutes to draw out the liquid.

2.

Meanwhile, sift the flours and baking powder into a large mixing bowl, add the lime zest and chilli flakes and mix briefly with a whisk. Bunch the nasturtium leaves together, roll into a tight tube and finely slice into very thin strips.
Add to the flour mixture.

3.

Wrap the courgettes in a clean tea towel and squeeze out as much liquid as possible. Add to the other ingredients in the mixing bowl, then add the peas, egg and milk, season with black pepper and mix well until you have a thick batter with no floury patches. Crumble in the feta, add the nasturtium petals and finally stir in the melted butter. Taste the batter and add a pinch more salt if necessary.

4.

Heat a large non-stick or seasoned cast-iron frying pan (skillet) or griddle over a medium-high heat. Once it is hot, add a tiny amount of oil – just a few drops – and spread it out carefully using a paper towel. Use a large spoon to dollop the batter into the pan, using a couple of spoonfuls to make each fritter. You will probably be able to fit three or four into the pan. Fry for 2–3 minutes, then flip and fry for a couple of minutes more. You will know they are ready to flip when small bubbles start forming on the uncooked side and the fritters don't feel sticky when you slide a spatula or fish slice underneath.

5.

Keep the fritters hot in a warmed bowl underneath a dish towel while you continue to cook with the rest of the batter, adding a little more oil to the pan if necessary. Serve warm with your choice of toppings.

NASTURTIUM CAPERS

Nasturtiums just keep on giving! Once the flowers have faded, the seeds that form are deliciously spicy flavour bombs and, when pickled, make an excellent substitute for capers. Pick the seeds when they are bright green and still firm (keep the dry, brown ones for planting next year). They typically form in clusters of three, so gently break them apart for pickling. Use them anywhere you would capers; they are delicious in a salsa verde, with smoked salmon or in a butter sauce with pan-fried fish. For the quantities in this recipe, you will need a 230 g (8 oz) jar with a tightly fitting lid.

You can also make this recipe with an equal quantity of wild garlic buds or seeds. The buds have a sweet, grassy, garlicky flavour while the seeds are punchier.

Makes one 230 g (8 oz) jar

100 g (3½ oz) nasturtium seeds

1 tsp salt

50 ml (2 fl. oz) cider vinegar or white wine vinegar

1 dill flower (optional)

1.

Start by sterilizing the jar and lid, following the instructions on pages 179–81. Pick through, wash and separate the nasturtium seeds and put them in the jar. Measure 50 ml (2 fl. oz) boiling water into a heatproof jug (pitcher), add the salt and stir well to dissolve, then add the cider vinegar.

2.

Put the dill flower (if using) on top of the seeds in the jar and pour over the vinegar mixture. Seal with the lid and store in a cool, dark place for 10 days before using. Once opened, store in the fridge. They will keep well for three months, probably longer, in the fridge.

VIOLA
Viola tricolor

& GARDEN PANSY
Viola × wittrockiana

Typically grown as
a hardy annual

Height and spread up
to 20 cm (8 in)

Sun or
partial shade

Sow in spring
or early autumn

Harvest flowers
almost all year round

Why we grow them – Violas and their larger, showier cultivated cousins the garden pansies are some of the most delicately beautiful edible flowers in our garden. All have a similar bloom, with two upper petals and three lower ones marked with nectar lines that guide bees to the centre and create the distinctive 'face'. Some also have distinctively delicious leaves, with flavours of menthol and cinnamon. They self-seed readily, and each new plant will have a new combination of flower colours.

How to propagate – Buying a 'six-pack' selection of pansy seedlings from a garden centre is a very simple way to start your viola obsession. Just make sure you cut off the first round of flowers after your purchase and eat only the later blooms, in case they were sprayed with pesticides at the garden centre.

We propagate violas and pansies from seed. It's very easy, if a little more time-consuming. We sow seed singly in modules or soil blocks in spring and early autumn for pretty much a year-round supply of flowers. Violas always seem incredibly slow to get going, but be patient, and if you keep picking a single plant can provide you with hundreds of beautiful flowers.

How to grow – If slugs or snails are a regular problem in your garden, growing violas or pansies in hanging baskets is a great option.

This is how we started, when we were struggling to get on top of the slug population in our newly made vegetable beds.

Many violas and pansies are technically perennial and will survive even very cold winters, but they are often grown as annuals because they can become straggly and unsightly after just one season. Although cutting them back hard can result in new growth, it as often as not kills the plant.

Collecting seed from violas and pansies is easy. We inevitably miss some flowers when deadheading and find a neat three-pointed star-shaped seed pod in its place a week or two later, packed full of tiny spherical brown or black seeds. Alternatively, dig up and move the tiny seedlings that will spring up all year round where pansies have been growing.

How to harvest – Harvest the flowers regularly to encourage more.

FLOWERS *April to December.*

DO *press the flowers for beautiful decorations for cakes and biscuits.*

DON'T *forget to have a nibble on the leaves.*

TASTES *mildly floral; some leaves have a distinctive cinnamon flavour.*

VIETNAMESE SUMMER ROLLS WITH EDIBLE FLOWERS

Vietnamese summer rolls are deliciously fresh and crisp, and with this zingy, spicy dipping sauce they make a perfect summer appetizer or lunch. Here we give the 'classic' recipe, with aromatic pork and sweet prawns (shrimp), but we've made all sorts of versions – try adding avocado, mango, pineapple, smoked salmon, roasted (bell) pepper or satay chicken, or using leftover roast chicken, beef or pork.

Adding edible flowers makes the rolls look gorgeous. We particularly love cheery violas because they look like sweet little faces, but calendula and dahlia petals also work well, and nasturtiums add bright colour and a little peppery flavour.

Makes 16 rolls

For the pork:

500 g (1 lb 2 oz) pork loin

1 tsp salt

1 tsp sugar

½ tsp Chinese five spice

4 garlic cloves, finely chopped

2 tbsp soy sauce

300 ml (10 fl. oz) vegetable or chicken stock (broth)

2 tbsp sweet chilli sauce

1 tbsp oil

1.

Rub the pork loin with the salt, sugar, five spice and garlic and place in a large bowl or tray. Leave to marinate for at least 30 minutes at room temperature, or refrigerate overnight.

2.

When you are ready to cook the pork, put the soy sauce, stock (broth) and sweet chilli sauce in a measuring jug (pitcher) or bowl. Scrape most of the garlic from the pork and add this too.

3.

Put the oil in a deep pan (for which you have a lid) over a high heat, then sear the pork on all sides.

4.

Pour the stock mixture into the pan, reduce the heat to medium, cover and simmer for 30–45 minutes, or until the pork is cooked through. It should feel quite firm when you push it, but if you are unsure just take it out and cut into the middle. If it is still pink, cook it for a little longer. You will be slicing it anyway.

5.

Take the pork out of the pan and set it aside to rest. Increase the heat and simmer the sauce to reduce it to a thick glaze. Pour it over the pork, leave to cool completely and put it in the fridge. It will be much easier to slice thinly when it is cold.

6.

Make the dipping sauce by combining the fish sauce, vinegar, sugar and lime juice, stirring well to ensure the sugar is completely dissolved. Add the garlic and the chilli flakes or chopped chilli.

7.

Put the noodles in a bowl and cover with boiling water. Leave to soak for 5–10 minutes, until soft, then drain.

8.

Now arrange all the other ingredients for the rolls so that you can easily reach them as you make the rolls. Slice the pork thinly and cut into rectangles approximately 5 × 3 cm (2 × 1 in). Cut the cucumber in half lengthways, scoop out the seeds with a small spoon and cut the flesh into matchsticks. Cut the spring onions (scallions) into 5 cm (2 in) lengths and then slice into fine strips. Pick the coriander (cilantro) into little sprigs and the mint into individual leaves.

9.

Dip one sheet of rice paper in a bowl of cold water for about 10 seconds, shake off the excess water and place it on a plate or board.

10.

Place a small amount of sliced lettuce, mint, coriander and noodles on the rice paper, 1 cm (½ in) in from the edge closest to you.

11.

Place a few batons of carrot, cucumber and spring onion next to the herbs and noodles.

12.

Next, beside the vegetable batons – you should now be about halfway up the paper – put a couple of edible flowers face down so that you can see the back of the flower or petal. Put a couple of prawns on top, arranging them so that you can see the prawns between the flowers. On top of this, add a few pieces of the sliced pork.

13.

Roll up from the edge nearest you until you reach the carrots, then fold in the sides and continue rolling to make a neat package. Serve as soon as possible, with the dipping sauce.

For the dipping sauce:

1½ tbsp fish sauce

1½ tbsp rice vinegar

1 tbsp sugar

1 tbsp lime juice

1 garlic clove, finely sliced

a pinch of chilli flakes (or 1 red chilli, finely chopped)

For the summer rolls:

50 g (1¾ oz) vermicelli noodles

half a cucumber

3 spring onions (scallions)

a small handful each of mint and coriander (cilantro) leaves

16 × 16 cm (6 × 6 in) circular rice paper summer roll wrappers

100 g (3½ oz) lettuce, finely sliced

1 carrot, peeled and cut into matchsticks

32 viola flowers

150 g (5½ oz) cooked prawns (shrimp), halved lengthways

EDIBLE FLOWER
COOKIES

These cookies are beautiful for a party or special afternoon tea, or as a gift, but this is also a fun project to do with kids. The key with most edible flowers is not to cook them for too long, because they go crispy and lose their colour and fresh appearance. For this reason, I add them when the cookies are almost completely baked. I often make these cookies using the dough from the German Cookies with Daisies (see page 164), adding the zest of a lemon to the dough and decorating with the flowers when the cookies are almost baked, as below.

For this recipe, we press the violas lightly so that they are flat and easy to put on top of the cookies. You don't need to press them for long, or until they are completely dried – just arrange between two sheets of clean paper, put a couple of heavy books on top and leave for an hour before using.

Makes 40–50 cookies using a 58 mm (2¼ in) cutter

180 g (6 oz) plain (all-purpose) flour

½ tsp bicarbonate of soda (baking soda)

1 tsp ground ginger

½ tsp ground cinnamon

½ tsp of freshly grated nutmeg

60 g (2 oz) cold butter, cubed

90 g (3¼ oz) light brown sugar

1 large egg, separated

2 tbsp golden (light corn) syrup

50 violas (or experiment with other edible flowers and leaves, such as primroses, honesty, cornflower petals, calendula petals, mint and lemon balm), gently shaken to remove any insects

sugar, for sprinkling

1.

Put the flour, sieved bicarbonate of soda (baking soda) and ground spices into a food processor. Add the butter and pulse until the mixture resembles breadcrumbs. Alternatively, put the dry ingredients in a large bowl and rub in the butter with your fingertips. Stir in the sugar.

2.

Add the egg yolk and golden (light corn) syrup to the ingredients in the food processor and pulse until the mixture clumps together. If mixing by hand, add it to the bowl and mix with a wooden spoon until it forms clumps.

3.

Bring the dough together with your hands and knead, briefly, on a lightly floured work surface until smooth. Wrap in a sandwich or freezer bag and refrigerate for 30 minutes.

4.

Preheat the oven to 180°C/350°F/Gas 4. Line a few large baking sheets with baking parchment or silicone mats.

5.

Roll out the dough on a lightly floured surface to a thickness of 2–3 mm (⅛ in). Cut into rounds using a fluted cookie cutter or an appropriately sized glass.

6.

Bake for 13 minutes. Take the cookies out of the oven and leave to cool completely; this will take only about 15 minutes, because they are so thin. Leave the oven on.

7.

Mix the egg white thoroughly with 1 tsp cold water, until it loses its gloopiness. Using a pastry brush, spread a little of the mixture on top of a cooled cookie, then arrange a flower carefully on top and brush with a little more of the egg white. Sprinkle with a little sugar. Repeat with all the cookies, then put them back in the oven and cook for 3 minutes. Cool on a wire rack before serving.

COLLECT SEED

Collecting seed from annual plants is a great way to share varieties and cultivars with neighbours and friends and build up a rich selection of seeds to grow in following years. We have found that it can be very simple and successful, particularly with annual edible flowers.

Unlike with cuttings (see page 294), the plants that grow from seed you've collected will not be genetically identical to their parents. This isn't cloning; seeds are the result of sexual reproduction, so genetic variation will occur. This can be a good or bad thing depending on whether you really like the characteristics of the parent plant or not, and in practice you will find that some things are better suited to being grown from seed than others.

How to save seed – As a general rule, it's much harder for pests and disease to be transferred from generation to generation when you collect seed than when you take cuttings, so you need not be too concerned with the pristine, healthy condition of the plant you're collecting from. In fact, I often find myself collecting seed from annual plants towards the end of their lives, so they are distinctly sad-looking, dried up and dying!

Ideally you should collect seeds when they are at the point of natural dispersal – when they are brown and mature and either just about ready to drop or already dropped onto the soil below. However, for ease of collection you can also pick them when they are still a bit green. They will stop growing once picked, but their seed coat should toughen up and mature.

I pick whole seed heads and put them in small wide bowls to dry (labelled, of course, with the cultivar if I know it or a description, such as 'Peachy with yellow middles', if I don't) in my garage – ideally somewhere breezy, out of direct sunlight and around 18°C (65°F). Once they are totally dry, break them up and pick out the chaff (material that isn't seed). Put the seeds in paper (or cloth) envelopes or bags. Label the containers and store them somewhere cool and dry. I add little sachets of silicone gel (the kind that come with new shoes) to suck up any residual moisture.

Seeds will keep for differing periods depending on species and conditions. All those mentioned in this book will last for several seasons, but I recommend collecting just a few each year since germination is always best with younger seed.

When not to save seed – If you are growing from seed a cultivar that is an F1 hybrid ('F1' will appear after the name: e.g. *Viola cornuta* 'Tiger Eye Red' F1), it is probably not worth collecting the seeds to grow again. F1 hybrids are created by crossing two plants from stable seed lines with different but very desirable characteristics. The first generation of plants from this (the plants you grew from the F1 seeds you bought) will have the desired combination of characteristics from the parents, but subsequent generations will not.

Similarly, there are some species for which it's not worth collecting seed unless you are an expert and have set up special controlled environments. Courgette (zucchini) flowers must be fertilized if they are to produce fruit (courgettes), but they can be fertilized by any closely related species. If you are growing squash and courgettes of various types, none of the next generation (assuming you let the courgettes grow huge, into marrows, then harvest the marrows, scoop out the seeds, dry them and save them for next year) will be anything like the courgette variety you started with.

Similarly, nasturtiums will interbreed with all the other nasturtium varieties nearby, so the seeds won't be true to the parent. However, I still collect nasturtium seeds and enjoy the pot-luck element of the next generation.

CHAPTER 2

Edible Borders

Korean mint & anise hyssop * Chives * Dahlia * Daisy *
English lavender * Green tulip * Primrose * Roman chamomile *
How to Press Flowers * Thyme * Wild garlic * How to Lift and Divide

This chapter is primarily about herbaceous perennials, leafy (non-woody) plants that typically die back to the ground each winter before springing to life again in spring.

Herbaceous is the opposite of woody. Woody plants, such as shrubs and trees, have a permanent structure that grows over time and survives from year to year. Herbaceous plants either die back to the ground in winter or are evergreen and provide year-round leafy ground cover. Perennials complete their life cycle in more than two years. Long-lived perennials may live for decades; short-lived perennials may survive for just a few years.

Herbaceous perennials are often planted in wide borders or beds, with the tallest at the back and low-lying specimens at the front, but even traditional borders like this can be edible as well as beautiful. These plants often spread over time and can be dug up in autumn or spring and divided (split into several plants) to keep them vigorous and create new plants for other parts of the garden, or to give to friends and family (see page 222).

This chapter also contains evergreen woody herbs (lavender, thyme), which can't be lifted and divided. But they are great in edible borders and can be propagated by taking cuttings (see page 294).

KOREAN MINT

Agastache rugosa

& ANISE HYSSOP

Agastache foeniculum

Hardy perennials

Height up
to 1.2 m (4 ft)

Spread up
to 0.5 m (1½ ft)

Full sun or partial shade,
well-drained soil

Sow or take cuttings in
spring/divide in autumn

Harvest flowers in late
summer and autumn

Why we grow it – When we discovered agastache – a relative of mint – it felt as though we'd taken our mint-growing to a new level. Korean mint and anise hyssop (or liquorice mint) taste of aniseed, mint and liquorice in various delightful combinations. You can justify growing either purely for aesthetic reasons, with their interesting foliage and tall spikes of purple flowers, but they are also beloved of bees and chefs equally.

How to propagate – If you find a small pot of agastache to buy, ask if you can taste a leaf before purchasing, and if you love it, take it home. Alternatively, it is easy to grow from seed. Sow in spring and pot on once the seedlings are big enough to handle, then plant out in clumps.

You can also propagate it by taking softwood cuttings in spring or by lifting and dividing the clump after flowering in autumn. However, agastache is far less vigorous than mint, and doesn't need to be lifted and divided regularly to stay healthy.

How to grow – Grow agastache in pots or in the ground. It doesn't spread very quickly, so plant groups of seedlings and in a few years they should bulk out nicely. It is happy in partial or full shade and likes well-drained soil, but it is unfussy.

How to harvest – Harvest the young leaves from late spring, and harvest young flower spikes all summer. Cut off whole tips to encourage bushy growth. The stems are tough, so pick off the young leaves and flower tip to use before composting the stem. The leaves become tougher and less aromatic as they age and increase in size.

FLOWERS *in late summer and autumn.*

DO *grow next to other Mediterranean herbs: chives, oregano and thyme.*

DON'T *leave it too late in the year to eat the leaves – they are most delicious when young.*

TASTES *like a combination of aniseedy Thai basil and mint.*

THE EDIBLE FLOWER

STIR-FRIED SPICY PORK WITH GARLIC SCAPES & ANISE HYSSOP

This is my interpretation of kaphrao (a stir-fried Thai dish flavoured with holy basil, chilli, soy, garlic and fish sauce), using anise hyssop in place of the basil. The flowering tops with their gorgeous purple flowers are delicious added to a stir-fry with the leaves. This recipe also uses garlic scapes, the flowering shoots of hardneck garlic, which are cut off before they flower to enable the plant to put all its energy into growing a delicious bulb.

If you can't get hold of garlic scapes, replace them with green beans and add a couple of finely sliced garlic cloves when you add the chilli and spring onions (scallions).

Serves 2–3 as a main dish

3 tbsp sunflower oil

50 g (1¾ oz) cashews

2 large red chillies, sliced at an angle

4 spring onions (scallions), sliced at an angle

300 g (10½ oz) minced (ground) pork

100 g (3½ oz) garlic scapes or green beans, cut into pieces 3 cm (1 in) long

100 g (3½ oz) mangetout (snow peas), trimmed, cut in half if large

2 tbsp soy sauce

1 tbsp fish sauce

1 tbsp palm sugar

a large handful of anise hyssop, leaves picked, flowering tops left whole

steamed jasmine rice, to serve

1.

You will need to work quickly once you start frying, so prepare all the ingredients first and have them to hand.

2.

Heat the oil in a wok over a high heat. Add the cashews and stir-fry for about 1 minute, until just turning golden brown. Remove them using a slotted spoon and set aside.

3.

Add the chillies and spring onions to the hot oil and stir-fry for about 1 minute, until starting to soften and smelling delicious. Add the pork and fry, stirring frequently, for about 3 minutes, until it has all changed colour. Add the garlic scapes or beans and the mangetout (snow peas) and fry for another 2 minutes, then add the soy sauce, fish sauce and palm sugar. Fry for another minute or two, until everything is slightly sticky and the sauce has reduced a little. Throw in the anise hyssop leaves and flowering tops and cook for another 15 seconds.

4.

Remove from the heat and stir in the fried cashews. Taste and add more soy or fish sauce if you like. Serve with steamed jasmine rice.

CHIVES

Allium schoenoprasum

Hardy perennial

Height up
to 0.3 m (1 ft)

Spread up
to 0.4 m (1¼ ft)

Full sun or partial shade,
well-drained soil

Sow in spring/
divide in autumn

Harvest flowers in late
spring/early summer

Why we grow them – Chives are
the most common of the numerous edible
perennial alliums that we grow here at
The Edible Flower. They are a ubiquitous
presence in herb gardens for good reason.
They are easy to grow, and their long,
hollow leaves and purple flowers are both
attractive in the garden and delicious in the
kitchen. Many people enjoy the leaves in
their food, but don't realize that the early
summer flowers are a very tasty alternative.

How to propagate – You can grow chives
from seed in spring, or buy a pot-grown plant
from the garden centre. Each year your clump
will get bigger, and you can lift and split it
every few years if you want to expand or create
a new patch.

How to grow – Chives are unfussy in terms
of location, but they like well-drained soil
and some sunshine. They can in fact thrive in
very poor soil, and will often spread around in
gravel beds, rubbly areas or the cracks between
paving. They self-seed readily, so cut off the

flower heads in midsummer if you don't want
this to happen. We chop back the whole plant
at this time each year and new leafy growth
appears quickly; in a good year we will get a
second flush of flowers in autumn, too.
Divide clumps in autumn to keep your chives
vigorous and get more plants.

How to harvest – Cut off whole flower
heads with scissors or secateurs. Pull the
individual chive flowers off the heads to
sprinkle on salads.

FLOWERS *in early summer and
sometimes again in autumn.*

DO *lift and divide every few years to
rejuvenate your plants.*

DON'T *let it go to seed unless you
want chive seedlings popping up around
your garden.*

TASTES *of mild onion.*

CHIVE FLOWER
& CHEDDAR SCONES

When a scone (biscuit) is perfectly made, jam and cream are just too distracting, and if you don't need jam that opens up a world of savoury scones.

1.

Preheat the oven to 220°C/425°F/Gas 7 and put a large baking sheet in to heat up.

2.

Whisk the flour, salt and baking powder in a large mixing bowl to break up any lumps. Rub in the butter with your fingertips until the mixture resembles fine breadcrumbs.

3.

Each chive flower head is made up of dozens of tiny individual purple flowers. Pick these off the heads and add almost all of them to the bowl, reserving a few for sprinkling. Add the paprika and three quarters of the Cheddar.

4.

Make a well in the middle of the dry ingredients. Add most of the buttermilk and combine quickly with a butter knife or with your hand in an open claw shape. Add a little more buttermilk if necessary to make a soft but not sticky dough. Tip the dough out on to a lightly floured surface and fold it over a couple of times to neaten. Try not to overwork or knead the dough, as too much stretching will make the scones tough. Pat the dough into a round about 24 cm (9½ in) in diameter and 3–4 cm (1–1½ in) thick.

5.

Working quickly, brush the dough with a little buttermilk and sprinkle with the reserved Cheddar and chive flowers. Dust a large knife with flour and cut the dough into eight wedges, as though you were cutting a pizza. I dust the knife with flour between cuts to ensure a clean edge, which will help the scones to rise evenly.

6.

Put the scones on the preheated baking sheet and bake for 20–25 minutes, until golden with a well-baked base. Cool on a wire rack and serve with butter. The scones are best eaten on the day they are made, but they freeze well: simply warm them from frozen in a moderate oven for 15 minutes to serve.

Makes 8 scones

400 g (14 oz) self-raising (self-rising) flour, plus a little extra for dusting

½ tsp salt

1 tsp baking powder

100 g (3½ oz) cold butter, cubed

12 chive flower heads

1 tsp smoked paprika

75 g (2¾ oz) mature Cheddar, finely grated

250–300 ml (about 8.5 fl. oz) buttermilk, plus a little extra to glaze

DAHLIA

Dahlia pinnata

Tender perennial

Height 0.3 m (1 ft) to 1.2 m (4 ft), depending on the variety

Spread up to 0.6 m (2 ft)

Full sun

Sow seed or plant tubers in spring

Harvest flowers in late summer and autumn

Why we grow it – Before they became famous for their spectacular blooms, dahlias were popular in Victorian Britain for their edible tubers. I've eaten the tubers of several cultivars, but I'm not a big fan; they are crunchy, even once cooked, and have a definite celery flavour. The cultivars do vary, so perhaps I just haven't found the right one yet! We primarily grow dahlias for a late summer display of joyful blooms, and to decorate cakes. But we also eat the petals.

How to propagate – The easiest way to grow dahlias is to purchase tubers and plant them in late spring. Find a cultivar that you like the appearance of and be sure to find out how big it is likely to get. They can grow very tall, and the larger cultivars will need some support.

The more you grow dahlias, the more you can regularly lift and split the tubers to get more plants. We also grow dahlias from seed, sowing in spring and planting out the seedlings in midsummer. The plants are smaller initially, but I have been surprised at how quickly they catch up with the tuber-grown plants.

How to grow – I plant out our dahlia tubers a few weeks after the last frost in spring. It's important to wait for the weather to start warming up before doing this. I grow dahlias in rows as part of the vegetable bed, and in big dedicated borders. Do deadhead regularly to encourage more flowers.

Dahlia tubers were traditionally lifted and divided in winter to protect the tubers from frost, but increasingly I think our winters here in Northern Ireland aren't cold enough to justify it. However, it does enable us to get lots more plants each year. Cut the foliage back after the first autumn frost, then dig up the tubers carefully, brushing off the soil and labelling them as you go. There's no need to wash them, but do remove any obviously dead or diseased parts.

After lifting, our tubers sit upside down in a cool, dry outbuilding to dry off for a couple of weeks before we stack them in crates, with newspaper around them. In spring we divide them with a clean, sharp knife before planting them out, making sure each tuber or clump of tubers has a nice section of the crown where growing 'eyes' will form. Cut off and compost any tubers that are squashy or rotten.

How to harvest – Cut off the flowers using scissors or secateurs.

FLOWERS *from late summer into autumn.*

DO *wait until after the last frost before planting out.*

DON'T *forget to label your dahlia tubers when you lift them.*

TASTE *varies but flavours include lettuce, celery, chicory, apples and nuts. Often slightly bitter.*

ROASTED SWEDE
& GRAPE SALAD
WITH BLUE CHEESE
& DAHLIA PETALS

As late summer rolls into autumn, the dahlias continue to raise their vibrant, showy blooms, and yet my mind turns to more warming, substantial salads with earthy flavours and roasted roots. The slightly juicy nature of dahlia petals means they hold up perfectly when stirred through warm grains or pulses, and add a pleasing texture.

**Serves 4
as a light meal
or side dish**

500 g (1 lb 2 oz) swede (rutabaga)

olive oil

200 g (7 oz) puy lentils

1 bay leaf

100 ml (3½ fl. oz) white wine (optional)

1 tbsp cider vinegar

150 g (5½ oz) soft blue cheese, such as Cashel Blue or gorgonzola

200 g (7 oz) red seedless grapes

2 tbsp maple syrup

a pinch of chilli flakes

a handful of dahlia petals

salt and freshly ground black pepper

1.

Preheat the oven to 200°C/400°F/Gas 6. Peel the swede (rutabaga) and cut into 2 cm (1 in) cubes. Spread it out on a large baking tray (pan), drizzle with 1 tbsp olive oil, season with salt and pepper and mix well until coated. Roast for 20 minutes.

2.

Meanwhile, put the lentils, bay leaf and wine, if using, in a pan and cover with cold water. (I wouldn't open a bottle of wine especially for this recipe, but if you have one on the go it does add flavour.) Bring to the boil over a high heat with the lid on, then reduce the heat and simmer for 15–20 minutes, until the lentils are cooked through but holding their shape.

3.

Drain the lentils well and return to the warm pan. Stir in the vinegar and 50 g (2 oz) of the cheese and season with black pepper. Taste and add a little salt if necessary. Keep warm in the pan.

4.

After the swede has been cooking for 20 minutes, take the tray out of the oven and mix in the grapes and 1 tbsp olive oil. Cook for another 20 minutes, until the grapes are bursting and the swede is soft and starting to crisp and caramelize at the edges. Add the maple syrup and chilli flakes to taste, stir until coated and cook for a further 5 minutes.

5.

Stir three quarters of the dahlia petals through the lentils and put them on a large warmed platter or four individual plates. Arrange the swede and grapes on top and crumble over the remaining cheese. Sprinkle with the rest of the petals and serve.

DAISY

Bellis perennis

Hardy evergreen perennial

Height and spread up
to 10 cm (4 in)

Full sun or partial shade

Sow in spring

Harvest flowers from late
spring until autumn

Why we grow it – The enormous Asteraceae (daisy) family contains many beautiful edibles, including lettuce, sunflowers, dandelions, globe and Jerusalem artichokes, dahlias, calendula, chamomile, chicory and yarrow. It also contains the humble lawn daisy, which has just the right growth habit to coexist with grass in lawns. It also has a long flowering season, from spring through to autumn. When you spot daisies and other 'weeds' in your lawn, keep it herbicide-free: admire the bees and enjoy the fact that you can eat the flowers. Please note that some members of the Asteraceae family are toxic, so make sure you check the edibility of any flower before eating it.

How to propagate – If you have a lawn, you may be lucky enough to have a good supply of daisies without any additional effort. You can also grow daisies from seed sown in spring.

How to grow – You can grow daisies in flower beds or pots, as well as in the lawn. Being small, they work well in small pots or at the front of borders. They will self-seed, so I keep them out of the vegetable beds.

How to harvest – Pick the flowers by hand. You may want to include a long stalk if you are pressing flowers for cakes, or just pick the flower heads. Just because there are healthy-looking daisies in a lawn, you can't be sure that it hasn't recently been sprayed with herbicides or pesticides, so, as with all the flowers in this book, know what you're picking, and if in doubt, don't.

FLOWERS *in late spring, summer and into autumn.*

DO *eat the flowers fresh or pressed.*

DON'T *pick from areas where there is any risk of recent herbicide or pesticide spraying.*

TASTES *mild, with a little honey sweetness.*

THE EDIBLE FLOWER

GERMAN COOKIES WITH DAISIES

These cookies make my heart sing with their candy-coloured loveliness, and also because this is my nannie's recipe, and it reminds me of playing tea parties at her house. They are similar to German Linzer cookies. During World War I they were renamed Empire biscuits in England and Belgian biscuits in Scotland, but they stayed 'German' in Northern Ireland. You can use whatever jam you fancy to sandwich the cookies together. The flowers for this recipe must be fully pressed or they won't sit flush with the icing (frosting).

Order dried hibiscus flowers online or from Asian, Middle Eastern or Mexican supermarkets.

You can grow sorrel leaves, or forage for them if you know what you are looking for; they are also sometimes available in good greengrocers. They have a lovely lemony, green-apple flavour.

1.

Preheat the oven to 170°C/335°F/Gas 3½. Line two large baking sheets with baking parchment or silicone mats.

2.

Cream the butter and sugar in a stand mixer or by hand until well mixed, but not light and fluffy as you would for a cake. Sift the three flours together into another bowl, making sure they are well mixed. Add half the flour to the butter mixture and mix until incorporated, then add the rest of the flour and mix to a dough.

3.

If the dough feels soft, put it in a plastic bag or airtight box in the fridge for 15 minutes to firm up.

4.

Dust your work surface with cornflour (cornstarch) and roll out the dough until it is 2 mm (⅛ in) thick. The dough is quite delicate, so you may find it easier to divide it in half for rolling. Cut out cookies using a 6.5 cm (2½ in) cutter with a fluted edge, if you have one, or a suitably sized glass. Transfer the cookies to the baking sheets, spacing them 2 cm (¾ in) apart, then re-roll any scraps and cut out more cookies. (Be sure to make an even

Makes 12–14 cookies

For the cookies:

115 g (4 oz) butter, at room temperature

45 g (1¼ oz) icing (confectioner's) sugar, sifted

115 g (4 oz) plain (all-purpose) flour

30 g (1 oz) self-raising (self-rising) flour

30 g (1 oz) cornflour (cornstarch), plus extra for dusting

For the decoration:

a selection of flowers and leaves to colour the icing (frosting), such as dried hibiscus (pink), fresh sorrel (green), dried cornflower petals (blue and purple), gorse petals (yellow) or calendula petals (orange)

about 15 small pressed flowers, such as daisies, primroses and violas (see page 208)

150–250 g (5½–9 oz) icing (confectioner's) sugar, depending on how many colours you want to make

150 g (5½ oz) jam or jelly of your choice

number, otherwise you'll have one left after sandwiching the cookies together.)

5.

Bake for 15 minutes, until lightly golden. Check after 10 minutes and rotate the trays if the cookies are browning unevenly. Cool on a wire rack.

6.

Now choose your colours and make the icing. For pink, put a couple of dried hibiscus flowers in a jug (pitcher) with 2 tbsp boiling water, leave to infuse (steep) for 10 minutes, then strain. Put 50 g (1¾ oz) icing (confectioner's) sugar in a small bowl. Add the hibiscus water very gradually, a few drops at a time, mixing well after each addition, until you have a smooth but quite thick glacé icing. It's always best to add less rather than more liquid, as you can add a few more drops if you find it is too thick when you are icing the cookies. If the icing is too thin it will run off the sides of the cookies, but you can add more icing sugar to thicken it.

7.

For green, put a small handful of sorrel leaves in a food processor or blender with 100 ml (3½ fl. oz) water and blend until fully combined. Strain through a fine sieve (strainer), then gradually mix a few drops with 50 g (1¾ oz) icing sugar, as in step 6.

8.

For pale blue and purple, put 1 tbsp dried cornflower petals and 2 tbsp icing sugar in a spice grinder or small food processor and whizz together until powdery. Gradually add cold water, as in step 6.

9.

For orange, put 1 tbsp dried calendula petals and 2 tbsp icing sugar in a spice grinder or small food processor and whizz together until powdery. Gradually add cold water, as in step 6.

10.

Carefully dollop about 1 tsp icing on to the middle of half of the cookies; if it is the right consistency it will spread a little but not run off the edge. Working quickly, before the icing sets, put a pressed flower on top of each dollop of icing. When the icing is set, spread 1 tsp jam or jelly on the back of the un-iced cookies and carefully sandwich each with an iced cookie. These cookies are best eaten the day they are made, as the jam tends to make them a bit soggy after a while, but they will keep for a couple of days in an airtight container.

ENGLISH LAVENDER

Lavandula angustifolia

Bushy shrub

Height up
to 0.8 m (2½ ft)

Spread up
to 1 m (3¼ ft)

Full sun, well-drained soil

Take cuttings
in early summer

Harvest flowers
in summer

Why we grow it – English lavender is the most highly scented lavender of all, and the best for cooking. It's also hardier than some other species, so better suited to a colder climate. Used judiciously, it can be a brilliant addition to recipes. Its piercing herbal scent makes it a brilliant replacement for rosemary or thyme with lamb or roast chicken, but it is also fantastic with sugar, dairy, chocolate and stone fruit, so consider adding a sprig when poaching peaches or apricots.

How to propagate – Take softwood cuttings or semi-ripe cuttings (see page 294) in early summer, from healthy new growth that hasn't flowered yet. Pot on once the cuttings have rooted, and overwinter them in a greenhouse or on a windowsill before planting out in spring.

How to grow – Lavender loves sunshine but also, more importantly, hates sitting in waterlogged soil. I grow ours at the top end of a sunny, slightly sloping flower bed with other drought-tolerant Mediterranean herbs: rosemary, oregano, thyme, winter savory and sage. I even threw in several buckets of sand and bits of concrete to ensure good drainage before planting my herbs.

Plants with needle-like leaves, such as lavender, have evolved to minimize water loss. The shape (and silvery colour) of the leaf is an excellent clue that they are used to hot, dry conditions and will cope well with minimal watering, well-drained soil and plenty of sunshine.

Lavender does need annual shaping to avoid it becoming straggly and woody (as does its horticultural and culinary friend rosemary). Cut it back each spring into the desired shape, but don't cut into old wood because it will not grow again. You have another chance to reshape after it flowers in summer. If you inherit a really big, woody or straggly plant, there isn't much you can do to rectify the situation in terms of its shape. I recommend taking several cuttings to replace it.

How to harvest and prep – Harvest the flower spikes with scissors or secateurs when the majority of the buds are open, then pick off the individual flowers to use in recipes. Lavender dries very well and doesn't drop its flowers too much as it does so (see page 86).

FLOWERS *in summer.*

DO *use the flowers to flavour sweet or savoury dishes. Dry the flowers or press the flower spikes to preserve.*

DON'T *over-use. Lavender is a strong flavour.*

TASTES *floral, menthol with a really strong aroma, not dissimilar in culinary terms to rosemary.*

SLOW-ROAST LAMB WITH LAVENDER, LEMON & APRICOTS

Being similar to rosemary, lavender is a perfect partner for lamb, its clean, aromatic flavour cutting through the rich fattiness of the meat. I've paired it with sweet dried apricots and sharp preserved lemon for a roast that is as delicious with potatoes and vegetables for a Sunday lunch as it is with couscous or freekeh for a Middle East-inspired dinner party. I've used dried lavender, because this is a great spring dish to make with new-season lamb, before the lavender is in bloom. If you make it with fresh lavender, the flavour will be stronger, so reduce the amount to 3 tsp.

This dish is delicious served with Roasted Carrots with Lavender and Orange (see recipe on page 173), and with couscous or freekeh; spoon some of the lamb juices over the grains for extra flavour.

Serves 8

6 garlic cloves, finely chopped

50 g (1¾ oz) preserved lemon peel, finely chopped

4 tsp dried lavender (about 6–8 heads), finely chopped

75 g (2¾ oz) dried apricots, coarsely chopped

3 tbsp sweet chilli sauce or apple jelly

a couple of pinches of chilli flakes (optional)

2 tbsp olive oil

2.5 kg (5½ lb) lamb shoulder, off the bone

sea salt and freshly ground black pepper

1.

Start by making the marinade. Mix the garlic, preserved lemon peel, lavender, apricots and chilli sauce or apple jelly in a small bowl. (If you are using apple jelly, you can add a couple of pinches of chilli flakes for a bit of a kick.) Add 2 tsp salt, a generous grind of pepper and the olive oil, and mix well.

2.

Unroll the lamb shoulder and spread three-quarters of the marinade over the inside of the meat. Re-roll the shoulder and secure it with kitchen string to make a neat package. Spread the remaining marinade over the outside of the lamb and season with a little more salt. Wrap in a double layer of kitchen foil, with the final seam on top. The lamb will release lots of juices as it cooks, and you want to trap those in the package to keep it moist and delicious. You can prepare the lamb up to this point the day before and store it in the fridge overnight.

THE EDIBLE FLOWER

3.

Preheat the oven to 160°C/325°F/Gas 3. Put the lamb in a deep baking tray (pan) that fits it snugly and cook for 3½ hours, or until tender. Check once or twice during this time, and if the juices are escaping, re-secure the foil.

4.

Increase the heat to 200°C/400°F/Gas 6, open the foil package and cook for another 30 minutes to crisp up the outside. Leave to rest for at least half an hour somewhere warm before slicing to serve.

ROASTED CARROTS WITH LAVENDER & ORANGE

I cannot resist roasted carrots and nor, it seems, can anyone else. No matter how many I make in the vain hope that there will be leftovers for lunch the next day, they are always all eaten. This is the perfect side to the Slow-Roast Lamb with Lavender, Lemon and Apricots (see page 170), but it is so delightful that you could also serve it by itself for a light lunch or dinner, with lots of flatbread for mopping up the yoghurt. It is particularly good made with blood oranges when they are in season.

1.

Preheat the oven to 200°C/400°F/Gas 6. While the oven is preheating, put the hazelnuts on a baking tray (pan) and roast for 10 minutes until they smell toasty. Chop roughly and set aside.

2.

If the carrots are very slim you can leave them whole, otherwise cut them lengthways into long, thin pieces. Put on a baking tray, drizzle with the olive oil, add the coriander seeds and season well with salt and pepper. Toss to coat in the seasoning. Roast for 20 minutes.

3.

Meanwhile, combine the orange juice, honey and lavender in a small bowl and stir well to dissolve the honey. After the carrots have roasted for 20 minutes, stir the orange and lavender mix into the carrots. Roast for another 5 minutes, until the carrots are tender and ever so slightly charred at the edges.

4.

Put the yoghurt in a bowl, add the garlic and ½ tsp salt, and mix well. To serve, spread the yoghurt on a platter, heap the hot carrots and the orange segments on top and sprinkle with the hazelnuts and fresh coriander. Serve immediately.

If the yoghurt is a bit loose, I like to drain off a little of the liquid to make it really thick. Put the yoghurt in a fine sieve (strainer) or a standard sieve lined with muslin (cheesecloth) over a bowl and leave for at least half an hour to strain.

Serves 4 as a side dish, 2 as a main dish

30 g (¾ oz) blanched hazelnuts

750 g (1 lb 10 oz) carrots, scrubbed if small and peeled if large

2 tbsp olive oil

1 tbsp coriander seeds

30 ml (1 fl. oz) freshly squeezed orange juice (about half an orange)

20 g (¾ oz) honey (about 2 heaped tsp)

1 tsp fresh or dried lavender (the flowers from two heads of lavender), finely chopped

salt and freshly ground black pepper

For the yoghurt:

300 g (10½ oz) Greek (strained plain) yoghurt

1 small garlic clove, grated or very finely chopped

To serve:

1 orange, segmented or peeled and sliced

10 g (¼ oz) coriander (cilantro) leaves

LAVENDER SHORTBREAD

This extremely buttery shortbread lends itself beautifully to the fierce aroma of lavender. It is absolutely the easiest cookie to make, and minimal effort is required for maximum fragrant, crumbly reward. You can make it with dried lavender in winter or fresh in summer, or you can replace the sugar with lavender sugar (see page 269). This is the perfect cookie to go alongside a cup of tea, but it is also great cut into smaller squares and served with a dessert such as lemon posset or panna cotta.

Makes 35 cookies

315 g (11 oz) butter, cubed

350 g (12 oz) self-raising (self-rising) flour

120 g (4¼ oz) cornflour (cornstarch)

120 g (4¼ oz) caster (superfine) sugar, plus a little extra for sprinkling

½ tsp salt

1½ tsp fresh or dried lavender, very finely chopped

1.

Preheat the oven to 160°C/325°F/Gas 3.

2.

Melt the butter in a small pan over a medium–low heat, or in a bowl in the microwave. Sift the flour and cornflour (cornstarch) into a large bowl and stir in the sugar, salt and lavender.

3.

Add the melted butter and mix to a soft dough with a wooden spoon. You can use your hands to give it a quick knead and make sure there are no dry bits, but try not to mix it too much. Press the dough into a Swiss roll tin (pan) or similar baking tin measuring about 30 × 20 cm (12 × 8 in), and smooth out the top as much as possible; I find an offset spatula helps, but you can use your hands. There is no need to butter or line the tin – the mixture is so buttery it will not stick.

4.

Bake for about an hour, until just golden. Leave to cool for 10 minutes and then cut into fingers while still warm. Allow to cool completely before removing from the tin. Dust with caster (superfine) sugar and serve with a cup of tea.

QUINCE
& LAVENDER JAM

ENGLISH
LAVENDER

It makes me so happy to see shelves lined with
jars of glistening jewel-coloured jams and jellies,
and there is something particularly magical about
quinces. They smell of vanilla and honey and sweet
flowers, but are hard and bitter when uncooked;
add heat, sugar and time and they reveal their true
rosy-hued nature. If you don't have home-grown
quinces, you can often find them in Turkish or
Middle Eastern grocery stores. They are a perfect
match for floral flavours, such as lavender, rose or
German chamomile.

*If you are using dried rather than fresh lavender, the flavour may not
be as strong, so you may need to use a little extra.*

**Makes about
1.6 litres (2½ pints)
(or four 450 g/1 lb jars)**

1 litre (1¾ pints) water

juice of a large lemon

1 kg (2¼ lb) quince (about
4 large quinces)

650 g (1 lb 7½ oz) sugar

6 heads of lavender, very finely
chopped (about 3 tsp)

a couple of drops of olive oil

1.

Put a small plate in the freezer, to help you test the jam's set later.

2.

Wash and rinse four 450 g (1 lb) jars and their lids in hot water
and put the jars on a baking sheet. Put the lids in a small pan of
water and bring to the boil, then simmer for at least 10 minutes.

3.

Put the water and lemon juice into a large pan, at least 5 litres
(10 pints) capacity. A preserving pan is ideal if you have one.

4.

Peel and core the quince, then chop them into 1–2 cm (½–1 in)
cubes. Put the cubes into the water and lemon juice as you cut
them, to stop them discolouring. Bring the water to the boil,
then simmer for 20–30 minutes, until the quince is soft but not
falling apart.

5.

Preheat the oven to 140°C/275°F/Gas 1. Put the sugar in a heatproof bowl in the oven, to help it dissolve more quickly and reach setting point more quickly. At the same time, put the jars in the oven to sterilize.

6.

When the quince is soft, add the warm sugar and the lavender and stir until the sugar is dissolved. Increase the heat to high and cook for 15 minutes, then test to see if the jam is set.

You will know this jam is near setting point when it transforms from pale golden to a gorgeous rosy coral. If you see it changing colour, that is a good time to test if it's setting. Put a teaspoon of jam on the cold plate and return it to the freezer for a couple of minutes. If a wrinkle forms on the surface of the jam when you gently push your finger into it, the jam is set. If not, cook for another few minutes and test again. If you have a jam or cooking thermometer you will know your jam is set when it reaches 105°C (220°F), but I still always check with the cold plate to be absolutely sure.

7.

If there is any white or pink scum on the top of the jam, scoop it off, then add a few drops of olive oil and stir to dissolve the remaining scum.

8.

Take the sterilized jars out of the oven and pot up the jam using a sterilized ladle or funnel. Seal while still hot with the sterilized lids. The jam will last unopened for a year or more in a cool, dark place. Once open, store in the fridge and eat within a month. This jam is delicious on everything, but I particularly love it sandwiched in a sponge cake with vanilla buttercream icing (frosting).

GREEN TULIP

Tulipa viridiflora

Herbaceous perennial

Height up
to 30 cm (12 in)

Spread up
to 10 cm (4 in)

Full sun, well-drained soil

Plant bulbs in autumn

Harvest flowers in spring

Why we grow it – I've always loved tulips as a cut flower, but because they don't bloom reliably after their first season, I've always been too busy – and frugal – to buy and plant every season. Then we discovered green, or veridiflora, tulips (so called because most varieties have a green stripe on the outside of each petal). If you plant them deeply in the right spot they will flower year after year. All tulip petals are edible, not just those of green tulips, and they vary in taste but are generally quite mild. Ours are lettuce-like with a slight nutty sweetness.

WARNING: Don't eat the petals of any cut flowers you buy unless you're absolutely sure they are safe. They may have been sprayed with pesticides or herbicides that you definitely should not be ingesting.

How to propagate – Plant bought bulbs in mid- to late autumn for flowering the following spring, burying them to a depth at least three times the height of the bulb (five times the height is ideal). They should be planted about 10 cm (4 in) apart, so aim for 100 bulbs per square metre (10 per square foot). They must have well-drained soil or they will rot, so if you have heavy clay soil, put some grit in the bottom of the planting hole.

How to grow – If your clumps become overcrowded after a few years, lift and divide the bulbs after the leaves have died back, in mid- to late summer. I've yet to see this happen with ours – you need perfect conditions for this vegetative reproduction to occur.

If you don't eat all your tulip flowers, remove the seed heads after flowering and let the leaves die back before removing them. Try planting some half-hardy annuals, such as French marigolds, in the same area after your tulips finish, to hide the dying leaves.

How to harvest – Cut through the stem, leaving plenty of leaves so that the plant can continue to photosynthesize and replenish the energy stored in the bulb for next year. Keep the flower stems in a vase or cup of water until required in the kitchen. Gently push back each petal to remove it from the flower just before using.

FLOWERS *in spring.*

DO *eat the petals, raw, in salads and as garnishes.*

DON'T *eat other parts of the plant.*

TASTES *mild and lettuce-like. Some varieties taste much more floral than others.*

THE EDIBLE FLOWER

TULIP
SATAY SLAW

At The Edible Flower we make a lot of slaws.
They can be made with both summer and winter
vegetables, are a great way to use up a glut of
produce, and make a delicious prepare-ahead side
dish to almost everything. Tulips' crisp, juicy petals
make them the perfect edible flower for a slaw as
they are robust enough to hold up under the thick
dressing. The selection of vegetables given here
is just a guide, so feel free to use whatever you
have in the bottom of the fridge (or the garden).
Outside tulip season, dahlia and nasturtium petals
are excellent substitutes.

1.

Mix or whisk together all the dressing ingredients in a large bowl.

2.

Heat a frying pan (skillet) over a medium heat and toast the seeds
for a couple of minutes, stirring regularly, until they are just
starting to turn golden and smell toasty.

3.

Put the chopped vegetables, petals and herbs for the slaw into the
bowl on top of the dressing, reserving the garnishes. Mix well to
coat all the vegetables in the dressing. Transfer to a large serving
bowl and garnish with the remaining coriander (cilantro), radish
slices, tulip petals and the toasted seeds just before serving.

Serves 6 as a side dish

For the dressing:

2 tbsp smooth peanut butter

1½ tbsp soy sauce

1½ tbsp sweet chilli sauce

1 tbsp sesame oil

a generous pinch of turmeric

1 tsp finely chopped fresh
ginger

1 red chilli, finely chopped (or
to taste)

juice of half a lime

For the slaw:

2 tbsp mixed seeds (such
as sesame, pumpkin and
sunflower)

¼ small savoy cabbage, finely
sliced into long strips, avoiding
the core

¼ small red cabbage, finely
sliced into long strips, avoiding
the core

1 carrot, chopped into
matchsticks

6 radishes, thinly sliced into
rounds, reserving a few slices
to garnish

¼ red onion, very finely sliced
into half-moons

2 spring onions (scallions),
finely sliced

a couple of handfuls of tulip
petals (from about 8 tulips),
sliced, reserving a few petals
to garnish

20 g (¾ oz) coriander (cilantro)
leaves, roughly chopped,
reserving a few sprigs to garnish

SPICY THAI BEEF TULIP CUPS

Tulip petals are perfect for getting this sticky, spicy beef from plate to mouth, and I particularly love using bright red, orange and yellow ones for contrast with the green herbs. I serve all the elements in the middle of the table so that everyone can make their own, but you can also fill the petals in advance and serve them at a drinks party. This recipe is also delicious with minced (ground) pork, or a mixture of pork and beef, but whatever you use, choose meat with a high fat content for the most delicious result. If it isn't tulip season, use small lettuce leaves instead.

**Serves 4–6
as an appetizer**

1 tbsp sunflower oil

2 sticks lemongrass (or a handful of lemon verbena), finely chopped

25 g (1 oz) fresh ginger, finely chopped

2 red chillies, finely chopped, seeds removed if you like it less spicy

2 large garlic cloves, finely grated

500 g (1 lb 2 oz) minced (ground) beef, at least 15% fat

1 tbsp fish sauce

1 tbsp palm sugar or soft brown sugar

4 lime leaves, finely shredded

juice of half a lime, plus 1 lime cut into cheeks or wedges, to serve

25–30 large tulip petals

a small bunch of coriander (cilantro), mint and agastache or Thai basil leaves

50 g (1¾ oz) roasted, unsalted peanuts, roughly chopped

1.

Heat the oil in a frying pan (skillet) or wok over a medium heat. When it is hot but not smoking, add the lemongrass, ginger, red chilli and garlic. Stir-fry for about a minute, until they have started to soften and you can smell the aromatics.

2.

Add the beef and immediately increase the heat. Stir-fry for about 3 minutes, until the beef has changed colour and is almost cooked. Add the fish sauce, sugar and lime leaves and stir-fry for another couple of minutes, until everything is brown, a bit sticky and beginning to caramelize. Remove from the heat and add the lime juice. Taste and add more fish sauce or lime juice if necessary.

3.

Serve the sticky, spicy beef on a large dish surrounded by tulip petals, herbs, extra lime wedges and roasted peanuts. Using the petals as a cup, add the aromatic beef, herbs, peanuts and a squeeze of fresh lime, roll up a little to hold everything in, and eat.

THE EDIBLE FLOWER

PRIMROSE

Primula vulgaris

Semi-evergreen
perennial

Height and spread up
to 0.3 m (1 ft)

Full sun or partial
shade, moist soil

Divide in summer
or autumn

Harvest flowers
in spring and summer

Why we grow it – The sight of the first primrose in early spring is a joy each year. It's a happy reminder that longer days, warmer weather and a plentiful supply of fresh flowers and vegetables from the kitchen garden are not far away. Common or English primroses are a delightful, low-lying woodland-edge plant native to the UK and Ireland. Both flowers and leaves are edible, and they make a lovely addition to salads.

How to propagate – Primroses are a little tricky to grow from seed, so I recommend buying a plant or finding a friend who is willing to split one of their clumps with you. Dig up and divide large clumps every few years after flowering, in summer or autumn. Plant the divisions 30 cm (12 in) apart, and make sure the soil is kept moist while they settle in.

How to grow – Primroses like moist soil and some sunshine, but can definitely cope with summer shade. An ideal spot is underneath deciduous trees, for plenty of dappled sunshine in spring while they are in flower. Primroses are also excellent in pots. Deadhead your primroses to keep them flowering for longer. You can also remove dying lower leaves to keep the plants looking neat and reduce slug habitat.

How to harvest – Pick flowers by hand by pinching through the stem. Store in the fridge until you need them, and remove the sepals just before using.

FLOWERS *in early spring through to early summer.*

DO *use the young leaves and flowers in salads, and the flowers in desserts. Press the flowers to preserve them.*

DON'T *harvest without gloves if you have sensitive skin. The leaves may cause contact dermatitis.*

TASTES *mild, with a subtle honey flavour.*

PRIMROSE, PEA & RICOTTA TART

PRIMROSE

This tart is a celebration of the lovely late spring produce: peas, new-season greens, spring onions (scallions), mint, sorrel and delicate primroses. If you don't grow primroses, or if yours have finished by the time the peas are ready, replace them with violas for an equally gorgeous result.

**Makes one
26 cm (10 in) tart**

For the pastry:

100 g (3½ oz) wholemeal flour

100 g (3½ oz) plain
(all-purpose) flour

120 g (4¼ oz) cold butter,
cubed

1 egg, separated

1 tbsp very cold water

1.

First make the pastry. Combine the flours and a pinch of salt in a large bowl, and rub in the butter until the mixture resembles breadcrumbs. Add the egg yolk and water and bring the dough together with a butter knife. You can also do this in a food processor; add the butter on top of the flour and pulse a couple of times until the mixture resembles breadcrumbs, then add the egg yolk and water and pulse again until the pastry clumps. Reserve the egg white for use later in the recipe.

2.

Knead the dough for a couple of seconds, just until it comes together with no floury patches. Wrap it in cling film (plastic wrap) and refrigerate for 30 minutes.

3.

Preheat the oven to 190°C/375°F/Gas 5. Put the ricotta in a fine sieve (strainer) over a bowl to allow excess water to drip out.

4.

Heat the olive oil in a frying pan (skillet) over a medium heat and cook the spring onions until soft. Increase the heat and cook for another minute or two to evaporate as much water as possible from the onions. If you are using frozen peas, add them to the pan towards the end of this time, to defrost them.

5.

Put water in a small pan about 3 cm (1 in) deep and add the greens. Bring to the boil and cook for 3 minutes, then strain, wrap in a clean dish towel and squeeze out as much water as possible.

6.

Put the eggs and cream in a large bowl, add the greens, season with ½ tsp salt and lots of pepper, and blitz using a hand-held blender.

190

THE EDIBLE FLOWER

Alternatively, put everything in a regular blender. Stir in the chives, mint and sorrel. Taste and add more salt or pepper if necessary.

7.

Roll out the pastry on a lightly floured surface to a thickness of about 3 mm (⅛ in), into a circle large enough to line a 26 cm (10 in) loose-bottomed tart tin (pan) (3–4 cm/1½ in deep). Line the tin, being careful not to stretch the pastry. Don't trim the edges at this stage, unless there is a lot of overhang. Put a large circle of baking parchment on top of the pastry and fill with baking beans (pie weights) or uncooked rice. Bake for 20 minutes, then remove the beans or rice and bake for another 10 minutes. Finally, beat the egg white with a pinch of salt, brush it on to the inside of the pastry case and bake for another 5 minutes. Leave to cool a little, then trim the edges with a sharp knife.

For the filling:

200 g (7 oz) ricotta

1 tbsp olive oil

150 g (5½ oz) spring onions (scallions), finely chopped

100 g (3½ oz) fresh or frozen peas

100 g (3½ oz) roughly chopped de-stalked greens (such as spinach, chard, beetroot/beet leaves and a few primrose leaves), thoroughly washed

3 large eggs

150 ml (5 fl. oz) double (heavy) cream

25 g (1 oz) chives, finely chopped

25 g (1 oz) mint leaves, finely chopped

15 g (½ oz) sorrel, finely chopped (optional)

75 g (2¾ oz) Cheddar, grated

salt and freshly ground black pepper

25–30 primrose flowers, sepals removed, and 15 viola flowers, to decorate

8.

Turn the oven down to 150°C/300°F/Gas 2. Spoon the spring onions, peas, drained ricotta and grated Cheddar into the pastry case and pour over the green filling. Decorate the top with primroses and/or violas; I like concentric circles, but be creative. Bake for 35–40 minutes, or until the filling is mostly set but with a slight wobble in the middle. Leave to cool in the tin for half an hour. Serve slightly warm or at room temperature.

PARSNIP, HONEY
& PRIMROSE CAKE

I love to use the common primrose for this recipe, because I associate its delicate pale yellow so closely with late winter and early spring. Historically, parsnips and primroses have been a culinary pairing, undoubtedly because they are in season at the same time, although I think the subtle, honeyed sweetness of the primrose does complement the flavour of parsnips.

Serves 10

100 g (3½ oz) light brown sugar

75 ml (scant 3 fl. oz) honey

3 large eggs, at room temperature

200 g (7 oz) self-raising (self-rising) flour

1 tsp bicarbonate of soda (baking soda)

½ tsp salt

½ tsp ground ginger

½ tsp freshly grated nutmeg

100 g (3½ oz) sultanas (golden raisins)

200 g (7 oz) trimmed, peeled parsnips, finely grated

150 g (5½ oz) butter, melted and cooled slightly

1.

Preheat the oven to 180°C /350°F/Gas 4. Grease and base-line three 15 cm (6 in) cake tins (pans).

2.

Whisk the sugar, honey and eggs with an electric mixer or in a stand mixer on medium–high speed until combined, doubled in volume and very pale.

3.

In a separate bowl, mix the flour, bicarbonate of soda (baking soda), salt, ginger and nutmeg. Very gently fold the flour mixture into the egg and sugar mixture, until no dry, floury bits remain. Fold in the sultanas (golden raisins) and parsnip, then gently stir in the melted butter until just combined.

4.

Divide the batter between the three cake tins (about 350 g/12 oz in each), and smooth out. Bake for 25 minutes, or until a skewer inserted into the middle of each cake comes out clean. Leave to cool a little in the tins, then turn out on to a wire rack and leave to cool completely.

5.

Once the cakes are cool, make the icing (frosting). Pulse the sugar and primroses in a food processor until powdery. In a stand mixer, beat the butter until soft, add the primrose sugar and beat for another couple of minutes, until light and fluffy. Add the cream cheese and beat again until smooth. You can also do this by hand in a large bowl, but it will take much longer.

6.

Assemble the cake, spreading a thick layer of icing on top of each layer before adding the next. Spread a thick layer on top of the cake, then use a palette knife to create a nice swirl on top. Use a cocktail stick (toothpick) or skewer to make holes in the icing on top of the cake and gently push in the base of each primrose to create a lovely pattern.

If you don't have three 15 cm (6 in) round cake tins (pans), you can divide the batter between two 18 cm (7 in) round cake tins for a larger, double-layered cake. You may need to increase the cooking time by a few minutes.

For the icing (frosting):

100 g (3½ oz) icing (confectioner's) sugar

50 primrose flowers, plus another 10–12 of the prettiest primroses to decorate, sepals removed

100 g (3½ oz) butter, at room temperature

150 g (5½ oz) full-fat cream cheese

ROMAN CHAMOMILE

Chamaemelum nobile

Hardy perennial

Height and spread up
to 0.3 m (1 ft)

Full sun or partial shade,
well-drained soil

Sow in spring

Harvest flowers
in summer and autumn

Why we grow it – There is something undeniably romantic about a chamomile lawn. We have attempted to re-create some of that joy by planting Roman chamomile in the cracks of the concrete patio around our fire pit. The plants have established very well and are truly lovely, particularly when they brush against your feet and release their sweet, appley scent in waves. We use chamomile both pressed and fresh for decorating cakes and desserts.

How to propagate – Roman chamomile is easy to grow from seed. Sow the tiny seeds as thinly as you can on the surface of trays of compost in late spring, and prick out the seedlings as soon as they are big enough to handle. It is also possible to buy chamomile seedlings. Whichever method you choose, plant them out 10–30 cm (4–12 in) apart, depending on how quickly you want the plants to fill the space.

How to grow – Roman chamomile is generally easy to grow, but prefers a relatively sunny location in well-drained soil. It can also be grown in pots. Cut the plants back a couple of times each summer so that they don't become leggy. It will self-seed and spread readily. The seedlings with their distinctively feathery, fragrant leaves are easy to spot and pull out in unwanted locations.

German chamomile (*Matricaria chamomilla*) is a different species, that looks and smells very similar to Roman chamomile. It is an annual plant that is grown commercially for culinary chamomile. For tea and infusions, we find it has a better flavour – similar to Roman chamomile but without the bitter aftertaste. It is sown in spring and planted out at a spacing of 20 cm (8 in). Collecting seed is simple. Just pick the dying flower heads, dry them out and then rub them between your fingers to remove the chaff from the seeds. You can also start your German chamomile cultivation by sprinkling the contents of a chamomile teabag onto some compost in the spring.

How to harvest – Pick whole flowers by hand. Keep removing them to encourage more flowers.

FLOWERS *in summer and autumn.*

DO *position your chamomile where feet or hands will brush past it.*

DON'T *worry about drying the flowers before you make tea – you can use fresh flowers too. We find 10–15 heads of chamomile are enough to flavour a pot of tea.*

TASTES *like Turkish apple tea.*

THE EDIBLE FLOWER

THE EDIBLE FLOWER

CHAMOMILE
JELLIES

For me, chamomile tastes of crisp apples like Granny Smith, with a musky, grassy note underneath. Despite being a jelly, with all the connotations of children's parties, this is an elegant dessert. Being light enough to be a palate cleanser, it's ideal if you are planning to serve a cheeseboard afterwards. For a less complicated dessert, just make one layer – either the clear one or the milky one – and double the amount. Remember that this recipe requires lots of setting time, so ideally start the day before you want to serve it.

You will need four moulds that hold 160–200 ml (5–7 fl. oz) liquid (I use dariole moulds). If you are worried about turning the jelly out, make it in pretty, clear glasses instead, but reverse the layers so the clear layer is on top.

Serves 4

For the clear layer:

300 ml (10 fl. oz) water

2 tsp dried German chamomile flowers, or 2 tbsp fresh

30 g (1¼ oz) sugar

2 tsp lemon juice

3 sheets of gelatine

For the milk layer:

350 ml (12 fl. oz) full-fat milk

2 tsp dried German chamomile flowers, or 2 tbsp fresh

zest of half a lemon

30 g (1¼ oz) sugar

3 sheets of gelatine

fresh edible flowers or pressed Roman chamomile flowers, to decorate

1.

First make the clear layer. Put the water and chamomile flowers in a pan and bring to a simmer. Remove from the heat and leave to infuse (steep) for at least 30 minutes.

2.

Strain the liquid through a very fine sieve (strainer). If there are still bits of chamomile in the liquid, strain it again through a piece of muslin (cheesecloth) or a clean dish towel. Wash the pan and put the liquid back in.

3.

Cut the gelatine sheets into pieces, put them in a small bowl and cover with cold water. Leave to soak for at least 5 minutes.

4.

Add the sugar to the chamomile liquid, heat gently and stir to dissolve. Bring to a simmer, then remove from the heat. Add the lemon juice.

5.

Strain the water off the gelatine sheets and add them to the hot chamomile liquid, stirring to dissolve. Divide the mixture evenly between four moulds, allow to cool a little, then leave to set in the fridge for at least 4 hours.

6.

When you are ready to make the second layer, put the milk in a pan with the lemon zest and chamomile. Bring almost to a simmer, then remove from the heat and leave to infuse (steep) for at least 30 minutes.

7.

Strain the liquid using a very fine sieve (strainer), as before, using muslin (cheesecloth) or a dish towel as well if necessary. Wash the pan and put the milk back in.

8.

Cut the gelatine sheets into pieces, put them in a small bowl and cover with cold water. Leave to soak for at least 5 minutes.

9.

Add the sugar to the milky liquid, heat gently and stir to dissolve. Bring almost to a simmer, then remove from the heat. Strain the water off the gelatine sheets and add them to the hot milk, stirring to dissolve. Leave to cool for 30 minutes, to prevent it from melting the jelly layer below as you pour it on.

10.

Divide the mixture evenly between the four moulds, on top of the clear layer. Allow to cool, then leave to set in the fridge for at least 6 hours, or overnight.

11.

To turn out the jellies, put some hot (not boiling) water in a bowl. Hold one mould in the warm water for 3–10 seconds, until you see the edges starting to melt. Invert the mould over a plate, hold the mould tight against the plate and give it a little shake, and the jelly should unmould. If it doesn't, hold it in the warm water for a little longer. You can also use a sharp knife to loosen the edges of the jelly carefully from the mould. Decorate the jellies with fresh edible flowers or pressed chamomile flowers.

EDIBLE FLOWER CAKE WITH SWEET GERANIUM, BLACKCURRANT & VANILLA

Pressed edible flowers make beautiful, delicate decorations for cakes, and are special enough for a celebration cake or even a wedding cake. You can use them with their stems to create a flower garden-style decoration, as I have done here, or take them off their stems to create more abstract patterns. Do plan in advance, as flowers take a couple of weeks to press (see page 208 for full instructions).

This recipe could have gone almost anywhere in this book, because I use a range of pressed flowers and leaves for decorating cakes. Roman chamomile presses beautifully and looks gorgeous on a cake, but other favourites include lavender, calendula, daisies, violas and small, simple dahlias.

Serves 12–16

For the cake:

225 g (8 oz) caster (superfine) sugar

4 large sweet geranium leaves, roughly chopped

225 g (8 oz) butter, at room temperature

4 large eggs, whisked

225 g (8 oz) self-raising (self-rising) flour

2–3 tbsp milk

1.

Preheat the oven to 190°C/370°F/Gas 5. Butter and line two 15 cm (6 in) loose-based cake tins (pans).

2.

Pulse the sugar and geranium leaves in a food processor until the leaves are finely chopped and the sugar turns bright green.

3.

Cream the butter until smooth, using a stand mixer with the beater attachment, or a wooden spoon and a lot of effort. Add the geranium sugar and beat on low speed until it is combined, then beat on high speed for 3–4 minutes, until light and fluffy. This will take longer if you are beating by hand.

4.

Add a spoonful of the whisked eggs and beat on high speed until the mixture is smooth and combined. Keep adding the egg and beating until all the egg is incorporated. For the last couple of additions, add 1 tbsp of the flour as well, to stop the mixture from splitting.

5.

Fold in the rest of the flour. I use the stand mixer at very low speed, but you can also do this by hand. Mix in the milk. The mixture should be thick but still drop slowly from a spoon.

6.

Weigh the cake mixture equally into the two tins. Smooth the tops and make a small indentation in the middle of each to counteract a domed rise.

7.

Bake for 25–30 minutes, until the cake is just starting to come away from the edge of the tins and a skewer comes out clean. Allow to cool in the tins for about 10 minutes, then remove from the tin and allow to cool completely on a wire rack.

8.

Cut the cakes in half horizontally, as evenly as possible, so that you have four separate layers.

9.

Now make the buttercream. Using a stand mixer with the paddle attachment, beat the butter on high speed for 5 minutes.

10.

Sift in the icing (confectioner's) sugar in a couple of batches, along with the vanilla, and beat on low speed until incorporated. Turn up the speed and beat on high for another 3 minutes. Add half the milk or cream and beat again. If you need to, add the rest of the milk or cream; the icing (frosting) should have a spreadable consistency that still holds its shape. If there are too many big air bubbles, reduce the speed and beat on low for a minute or two.

11.

Fill a piping bag with three quarters of the buttercream. Dot a little buttercream on to the plate or cake stand you are using. (The cake will need refrigerating after the first coat of buttercream, so make sure the plate or stand fits into the fridge.)

For the buttercream icing (frosting):

225 g (8 oz) butter, softened

550 g (1 lb 3¾ oz) icing (confectioner's) sugar, sifted

2 tsp vanilla bean paste, or the seeds from one vanilla pod (bean)

2–4 tbsp whole (full-cream) milk or single (light) cream

200 g (7 oz) blackcurrant jam or another jam of your choosing

To decorate:

pressed edible flowers, about 30–40 stems (see page 208)

fresh edible flowers and leaves (optional)

12.

Put the first cake layer on the plate, remembering how the next layer lines up. Pipe on a swirl of buttercream and use a palette knife to spread it out about 1 cm (½ in) thick. Now pipe a thin circle of buttercream around the top, about 0.5 cm (¼ in) in from the edge. This will be a barrier, to keep the jam from leaking out. Spoon one-third of the jam inside that line and spread it out.

13.

Repeat with the other layers. For the top two I always turn the cakes upside down, so that I end up with a bottom layer on the very top – this gives a cleaner edge.

14.

Once all the layers are assembled, do the crumb coat. This is a layer of icing that locks in the crumbs and evens out the surface before you do the final coat of icing. Pipe a zigzag of icing all the way around the cake, taking the zigs and zags to the top and bottom of the cake. Then use a palette knife to spread it out. Some areas will be thicker than others; the idea is to create a smooth cylinder of cake, filling in any gaps and imperfections. Finally, spread icing on top of the cake. Make sure the whole cake is covered in icing and there are no bare patches. Refrigerate the cake for 2 hours (or overnight) to set the icing.

15.

Beat the remaining buttercream again for a couple of minutes until it is soft and creamy and will spread easily. Using a palette knife, spread it over the sides of the cake in an even layer, then smooth the surface using the palette knife or a cake scraper, if you have one. Dollop the last of the buttercream on top of the cake, use the palette knife to spread it out and then create a swirl on the top of the cake.

16.

Now the fun begins. Arrange the pressed flowers on a work surface and start to select flowers to decorate the cake. To attach a pressed flower to the cake, hold it gently against the buttercream and press it in very lightly. Add flowers until you have decorated all the way round the cake and are happy with the result. If you want to reposition a flower, just peel it off and smooth out the icing using the warmed palette knife.

17.

Keep the cake in a cool room until you are ready to serve. Just before serving, you can decorate the top with fresh edible flowers and leaves. For larger flowers, use a cocktail stick (toothpick) or narrow skewer to make a hole in the top of the cake and gently push the flower stem in to hold it in place.

PRESS FLOWERS

Pressing edible flowers is a useful way to preserve blooms when they are at the height of their beauty, for later use. When you press flowers you are both drying and flattening them, and when fully pressed they will last almost indefinitely, as long as they are kept dry, although the colour may fade over time. It's very easy to do, and you don't need any special equipment, although if you are going to press a lot of flowers I recommend making or buying a flower press.

1.

First gather your materials. If you don't have a flower press, use a large book. Try not to use an old, dusty one, or at least give it a good dust before you use it – remember the flowers you press will be decorating food. You will also need a pile of heavy books to put on top of the book you are using as a press; all the books should be a similar size, to ensure even pressure.

You will also need clean sheets of paper to arrange the flowers on before pressing. I find that A4 recycled printer paper works very well, but you can also use sheets of baking parchment, which, with its silicone coating, makes the flowers less likely to stick as they press. Some people use fabric for pressing flowers, which helps with moisture absorption. Don't use anything with a textured surface unless you don't mind the texture imprinting on to the flower as you press it.

2.

Pick the flowers you want to press. They must be completely dry when you pick them, and ideally fully open.

3.

Arrange the flowers face down on a sheet of paper inside your press or book. If they have lots of petals, like calendula or daises, push them down a little so the petals aren't squashed underneath. If you are pressing flowers for

cookies, remove the stalk before pressing, but if you are pressing them for a cake decoration, leave the stalks on – you can trim them later.

4.

Put another sheet of paper on top of the flowers and close the book or put another sheet of cardboard on top in the flower press. Continue filling sheets of paper with flowers and layer inside the press or space them out inside the book.

Through trial and error, I've found that some edible flowers and leaves press better than others. Anything too thick or fleshy doesn't press well, because there is too much moisture. Similarly, some flowers and leaves seem to lose their colour more than others as they press. I've included a list of my favourites here.

5.

If you are using a book, close it and weigh it down with more books. If you are using a flower press, put the final layer of cardboard on top, followed by the top layer of the press. Assemble the bolts, tightening opposite corners together to ensure even pressure. After a day or so you will easily be able to retighten the bolts, so there is no need to overdo it at the start.

6.

Put the books or flower press in a warm, dry place. If the flowers get damp they can easily go mouldy.

7.

Allow the flowers to press for a couple of weeks before checking them. Bigger, moister flowers such as calendula and dahlia will take at least two weeks to press. Smaller, dryer flowers such as violas or lavender can press in as little as five days, but err on the side of caution to begin with, until you get a feel for it. A flower press will take a bit less time than a book because there is more air circulation inside, allowing the flowers to dry out more quickly.

8.

Once the flowers are fully pressed and completely dry, take them out of the press or book to store

them. I keep them between the sheets of paper I've used to press them, and store them in a box file in a warm, dry place. If any look mouldy, discard them.

Some of my favourites for pressing are:

* **Calendula** – Particularly the simple orange variety; the colour lasts very well

* **Cornflowers** – They press beautifully, but sometimes the blue colour fades a bit. Press whole flowers for cakes or individual petals for decorating cookies

* **Mustard flowers** – Pick stems with several flowers on to press

* **Sweet rocket flowers** – Press individual flowers, which look like little damselflies

* **Violas** – They keep their colour beautifully. I also press the leaves

* **Roman chamomile** – For the best look, detach the stalk from the flower head and press them separately, then reconstruct them on the cake

* **Primroses** – They keep their colour beautifully and work well on cakes and cookies

* **Daisies** – Press with their stalks for cakes or without for cookies

* **Lavender** – Press whole stalks to decorate cakes

* **Dahlia** – The simple 'Piccolo' type presses well for cakes and looks very dramatic. Larger dahlias with lots of petals don't press well

* **Nasturtiums** – You can press the leaves as well

* **Honesty** – Individual flowers or small sprigs press well, with a beautiful purple that fades over time.

THYME

Thymus vulgaris

Small bushy shrub

Height up to 0.4 m (1¼ ft)

Spread up to 0.6 m (2 ft)

Full sun, poor,
well-drained soil

Sow seed or take cuttings
in spring

Harvest flowers
in early summer

Why we grow it – Thyme is an underrated and underused herb in the kitchen and garden, perhaps because of its woodiness and the fiddly job of removing the tiny leaves. But those leaves provide an amazing punch of fragrance and a special flavour. We use fresh thyme leaves and flowers as a substitute for basil (with tomatoes and other ingredients) before that crop gets going later in summer. As with many woody herbs, thyme flowers taste similar to the leaves, and are beloved of bees.

How to propagate – The quickest way is by buying a small plant, but I've grown thyme successfully from seed and from softwood cuttings (the latter is useful if a friend or neighbour has a particularly nice variety). Sow seed in pots any time from early spring to early summer, and plant the seedlings out once they are large enough to handle. They will be slow to get going but should spread nicely in their second year. Take softwood cuttings from new growth in spring.

How to grow – Thyme is a tough little plant and requires little maintenance in return for a continuous supply of fragrant leaves and a summer burst of purple flowers. It thrives in sunny, dry conditions but is also very hardy and tolerant of freezing temperatures. To stop the plant getting straggly, cut it back after it flowers each summer. If you forget, you can also cut it back in spring, but don't cut into the previous season's woody growth as it won't regrow.

How to harvest and prep – Cut off a sprig of flower heads or leaves with scissors. Pick off the flowers and leaves by hand.

FLOWERS *in early summer.*

DO *plant alongside other sun-loving, drought-tolerant herbs such as oregano, rosemary, sage and lavender.*

DON'T *forget to cut it back after it flowers.*

TASTES *of thyme!*

HONEY-GLAZED HALLOUMI PANZANELLA WITH THYME

Tomatoes, halloumi, good bread – what's not to like? The honey-and-thyme-glazed halloumi is very special, and the purple-pink thyme flowers add beauty and flavour.

1.

Preheat the oven to 180°C/350°F/Gas 4. Put the tomatoes in a bowl, toss with a couple of generous pinches of sea salt and leave for 15 minutes to release their juices.

2.

Put the shallot or red onion and vinegar in a small bowl to pickle lightly. This will make the onion taste a little milder.

3.

Put the bread on a baking sheet, add 1 tbsp of the olive oil and a pinch of salt, stir to combine and cook in the oven for 10 minutes, until just turning golden.

4.

Add the warm bread to the bowl with the tomatoes. Add 2 tbsp of the olive oil, the shallot/onion and vinegar mixture, the garlic and the basil or anise hyssop. Mix gently, then set aside.

5.

Mix the honey, lemon juice and thyme leaves in a small bowl. Heat a large non-stick frying pan (skillet) over a medium heat, add the remaining 1 tbsp olive oil and fry the halloumi for a minute on each side, until golden brown. Add the honey and lemon mixture; it should bubble up and reduce. Turn the halloumi in the honey mixture until coated.

6.

Put the tomato and bread salad in a bowl, arrange the halloumi on top and sprinkle with the thyme flowers. Serve immediately, while the halloumi is still hot and crispy.

Serves 4
as an appetizer or as a main with other dishes

500 g (1 lb 2 oz) ripe tomatoes, cut into chunks if large, halved or quartered if small

1 large shallot or ¼ small red onion, finely sliced

1 tbsp red wine vinegar

100 g (3½ oz) ciabatta or sourdough bread (a couple of days old is best), cut or torn into 2 cm (1 in) chunks

4 tbsp olive oil

1 small garlic clove, crushed to a paste or finely grated

15 g (½ oz) basil or anise hyssop leaves, torn or finely shredded

1 tbsp honey

2 tsp lemon juice

leaves from a couple of small sprigs of thyme

250 g (9 oz) halloumi, cubed

sea salt and freshly ground black pepper

1 tbsp thyme flowers, to garnish

WILD GARLIC

Allium ursinum

Herbaceous perennial

Height up to 0.3 m (1 ft)

Spread up to 0.2 m (8 in)

Full or partial shade, moist soil

Sow seed or divide in spring

Harvest flowers in late spring

Why we grow it – Wild garlic (also known as ramsons) is normally the food of foragers. It is a spring treat here at The Edible Flower, and it usually pops up just after our three-cornered leek, long after our stored garlic bulbs have been eaten and shortly before our overwintered spring onions (scallions) are getting going. Rather than forage, we have created a wild garlic patch in a shady, unused corner. We love eating the leaves, the buds, the star-shaped flowers and the seed heads.

How to propagate – We have found it hard to find wild garlic seeds for sale. However, it is possible to grow it from seed, if you collect the seeds from the small seed heads and sow in early spring. I would suggest growing the seedlings on in pots for one season before planting them out.

We were lucky enough to be able to dig up clumps of wild garlic from a friend's woodland (the area was about to be turned into a path). We split the clumps and planted the divisions in a grid, leaving 10 cm (4 in) between plants. After just one year they were bunching up nicely and we were harvesting the occasional leaf and the flowers.

How to grow – One of the joys of foraging is that you get to understand the conditions in which the plant thrives by simply observing where it appears in great numbers. I have only ever seen wild garlic in damp, shady woodland areas, and that is what we have re-created for our wild garlic at home. Choose your location wisely. If conditions are good, your wild garlic will spread over time and be very tricky to get rid of.

The only slightly difficult aspect is weed control when your wild garlic patch is getting established. I suggest using some form of light exclusion for a year or two before planting, to kill off all weeds in the area. We planted our wild garlic under a tree where we used to have some large compost heaps. We scraped off the last of the compost to reveal beautiful weed-free compost-rich soil, and planted the wild garlic straight into that. The weeds will return eventually, but by then the garlic will have had a very good start.

How to harvest – Harvest the leaves individually by hand, just a few from each plant. Cut off the flowering stems with secateurs or scissors.

Rules for sensible and responsible foraging:
* *Never pick or eat anything that you're not totally certain about in terms of identification*
* *Never pick from areas where dogs are likely to have peed*
* *Wash your foraged food very thoroughly before use*
* *Never pick more than you need*
* *Never dig up a plant without permission from the landowner.*

FLOWERS *in late spring.*

DO *take just a few leaves from each plant.*

DON'T *dig up any wild garlic without permission from the landowner.*

TASTES *of garlic but more mellow and grassy.*

THE EDIBLE FLOWER

WILD GARLIC MALFATTI WITH RICH TOMATO SAUCE & TOASTED WALNUTS

This recipe is a bit of a cheat, being more about the wild garlic-leaf dumplings than the flowers, but it's delicious and relatively easy to make, and the flowers do make a stunning garnish. Wild garlic flowers and leaves are also brilliant in homemade pasta (see page 106), or use them instead of chive flowers in scones (see recipe on page 155). The base tomato sauce for the dumplings is based on Marcella Hazan's classic tomato sauce recipe, which is a perfect showcase for these garlicy malfatti.

Makes 20 dumplings

400 g (14 oz) can chopped tomatoes

half an onion, peeled, roots trimmed

30 g (1¼ oz) butter

200 g (7 oz) wild garlic

250 g (9 oz) drained ricotta

1 egg

75 g (2¾ oz) grated Parmesan, plus extra to serve

50 g (1¾ oz) Italian 00 flour or plain (all-purpose) flour

1 tsp freshly grated nutmeg

50 g (1¾ oz) polenta (cornmeal) or semolina

salt and freshly ground black pepper

30 g (1¼ oz) toasted walnuts, broken into small pieces, to garnish

a small handful of wild garlic flowers, to garnish

1.

First make the tomato sauce. Put the tomatoes, onion and butter with a pinch of salt in a small pan over a medium heat. Bring to the boil, then simmer for half an hour.

2.

Meanwhile, make the dumplings. Put about 2 cm (1 in) of water in a medium pan, cover and bring to the boil. Add the wild garlic and leave to steam, covered, for 3 minutes. Drain and leave until cool enough to handle, then squeeze the leaves really well in your hands or a clean dish towel to wring out as much water as possible. Chop finely.

3.

Put the ricotta, egg, wild garlic and Parmesan in a large bowl and mix well. Add the flour and nutmeg, if using, and mix again. Add black pepper and then taste, adding more salt, pepper and nutmeg as required.

4.

Put the polenta (cornmeal) or semolina on a baking sheet lined with baking parchment or a silicone mat. Roll the ricotta mixture into walnut-sized balls and gently roll in the polenta or semolina to coat. Sit them on the polenta-covered tray while you roll the rest of the mixture; you should get about 20 dumplings.

5.

When the tomato sauce is ready, remove and discard the onion. Use a hand-held blender to whizz the sauce to a smooth consistency.

6.

Bring a large pan of water to the boil and add 1 tsp salt. (If you don't have a large enough pan, cook the dumplings in two batches.) Carefully add the dumplings to the boiling water, stir gently to make sure they don't stick to the bottom of the pan, and cook for 3–4 minutes. You will know they are ready when they bob to the surface. Gently remove the dumplings from the water using a slotted spoon, and drain in a sieve (strainer) or colander to let them steam dry.

7.

Put the warm tomato sauce in individual bowls, arrange the dumplings on top and sprinkle with the toasted walnuts, more grated Parmesan, black pepper and the wild garlic flowers.

LIFT & DIVIDE

Many herbaceous perennials will benefit from being 'lifted and divided' every few years. It helps the plants stay vigorous and healthy, and you get new plants to swap with friends. This technique involves carefully digging up the plant, splitting it into a number of plants, and then replanting them with adequate space between them to encourage further growth.

This should be done when the plant is dormant, typically in early spring or late autumn. As a rule, if the plant flowers early in the season, lift and divide in autumn after the flowers have died back; if the plant flowers late in the season, lift and divide in the spring.

1.

Carefully dig up the plant with a garden fork (if the plant is massive, you can dig up a corner of the plant and slowly work your way towards the centre). This is inevitably a stressful process for the plant, so pick a suitable time and day — a cool, still morning is ideal.

2.

For some plants, such as primroses or wild garlic, you will be able to split the clump into many little plantlets by hand. For more fibrous rooted plants, you may need to use two garden forks, inserted back-to-back into the centre of the clump, to prise it apart before breaking it up further by hand. For some plants, a sharp knife will be the easiest way to split up the mass of roots into smaller pieces.

3.

Replant the new plantlets immediately, either in the ground or into pots. (Don't leave them sitting in direct sun or strong breezes). Water them well and make sure they don't dry out over the next few weeks. The process will have inevitably damaged some roots and it will take time for the plants to settle into their new locations.

CHAPTER 3

Trees & Shrubs

Beach rose ✳ Elder ✳ Hawthorn ✳ Lilac ✳ Saucer magnolia
✳ Sweet geranium ✳ How to Take Cuttings

The plants in this chapter are all woody (i.e. not herbaceous) perennials, otherwise known as trees and shrubs. Trees and shrubs are woody perennial plants – that is to say, they have woody branches that survive above ground from year to year, either with leaves in winter (evergreen) or without (deciduous). Trees typically have a single stem from ground level and are bigger than shrubs, but it's not always clear what is a tree and what is a shrub.

It's often said that the ideal time to plant a tree is twenty years ago. There is inevitably a tension between getting on with actually planting trees and shrubs that may take some years to fulfil the purpose you have chosen for them – whether it's bountiful harvests of flowers or fruit, acting as a windbreak or hedge, creating privacy or shade for a seating area in your garden – and taking time to do the necessary planning and preparation to pick the right tree for the location. You can, of course, buy large specimens, but if, like me, you have many trees to plant and a minimal budget, buying very small, affordable bare-root plants (or taking cuttings, or growing from seed) and waiting several years for them to grow is the best option.

Whether you are buying young and small or mature and large, find out the final height and spread of the species and the cultivar, and mark it out in the space before purchasing. Then research what you need to do in terms of initial shaping or pruning to set up your shrub or tree for a lifetime of good harvests and admiring glances.

BEACH ROSE

Rosa rugosa

Deciduous,
suckering shrub

Height and spread up
to 2 m (6½ ft)

Full sun or partial shade,
well-drained or even sandy soil,
tolerant of wind and salt

Plant in early winter
or early spring

Harvest flowers from
late spring to early autumn

Why we grow it – All rose petals are edible, but those of *Rosa rugosa* are always our choice. This rugged, trouble-free, salt-tolerant rose forms dense thickets that make it ideal for hedges or windbreaks. It has highly scented pink or white flowers, and also provides a second harvest – of large dark-orange and red rosehips. We harvest petals from many roses, but we only ever bother harvesting hips from this one.

How to propagate – You can buy bare-root plants of *Rosa rugosa* in winter, when it is dormant. Plant out in early winter or early spring, when the ground isn't frozen or waterlogged. You can also remove suckers from a friend or neighbour's plant. Detach each sucker by using a spade to cut through the stem that attaches it to the parent plant, and repot it or plant it elsewhere. As with all bare-root plants or suckers that you've just dug up, don't leave them sitting out of the ground exposed to cold or drying winds. Keep them protected in a bag or bucket until you are ready to plant them properly.

How to grow – Pick your location wisely: *Rosa rugosa* gets big and will spread over time. Either clear the weeds from the area before planting by covering it with black plastic for a year, or, if you haven't thought that far ahead, dig out the weeds by hand or plant the rose through a thick mulch of cardboard covered in compost, manure or wood chips to give it a head start. For a really good, dense windbreak with the added bonus of delicious petals and hips, plant *Rosa rugosa* in a double row of five plants

to a metre (yard). *Rosa rugosa* doesn't need much maintenance but can be cut back with hedge trimmers to keep the size down for ease of harvesting.

How to harvest – You can harvest the whole flower with secateurs (be careful of the prickles), but our preferred method is to grab all the petals from one rose and gently pull them off. Assuming the flower has already been pollinated, it will continue to form a rose hip and you will be able to enjoy that too, later in the season. Aphids can sometimes be a problem on roses, so avoid harvesting aphid-laden flowers or remove the insects carefully after harvesting.

Often a single plant will have both flowers and hips available for harvesting at the same time. To harvest hips, cut them off with secateurs. All rose hips contain seeds, which are an irritant (a common ingredient in DIY itching powder, in fact) and must be removed before eating. We do this by cooking down the whole hip, then passing the resulting purée through a sieve (strainer) twice, to be sure all seeds and hairs are removed.

FLOWERS *in late spring to early autumn.*

DO *use the petals fresh or dried to make syrups, cordials, infusions and jellies.*

DON'T *ever, ever eat a whole hip. The seeds are extremely itch-inducing and it will be very unpleasant.*

TASTES *sweetly fragrant, of roses.*

ROSE WATER, SYRUP & JELLY

Rose water was traditionally a by-product of the process of extracting rose oil for perfumes and religious use, but it is now produced purely for culinary and cosmetic use, mostly in the Middle East (particularly Iran), through double steam distillation. Damask roses (*Rosa × Damascene*) are generally used for commercial production because of their excellent fragrance, but we find *Rosa rugosa* (which also has a wonderful scent) makes a great substitute.

1.

To make the rose water, you need a deep pan with a lid, ideally a lid that is slightly domed. Put a heatproof trivet in the bottom of the pan (I use a small metal bowl as my trivet). Add the rose petals and the water around the trivet, then put a small heatproof bowl on top of the trivet. There should be plenty of space between the edge of the bowl and the sides of the pan for steam to rise.

2.

Set the pan over a high heat with the lid on upside down (so the domed side is facing inwards). When the water starts to boil, reduce the heat so that the water simmers gently, and put an ice cube on the lid in the dip of the dome. Simmer for about 30 minutes, replacing the ice cube every 10 minutes. The volatile oils in the rose petals will be trapped in the steam that rises, and will condense when it hits the cold lid and drip back down into the small bowl.

3.

After about 30 minutes, remove from the heat. You will have about 100 (3½ fl. oz) rose water in the small bowl. Don't be tempted to keep cooking for more rose water; in my experience, this makes the water more dilute. Decant the rose water into a small jar or bottle for use in recipes such as the Spiced Chicken B'stilla Triangles (see page 236).

4.

Leave the rose petals sitting in the remaining water for another few hours, then strain though a piece of muslin (cheesecloth) to remove the petals and any other little flecks of dirt or pollen. You can now use this liquid to make rose syrup or rose jelly.

For rose water:

Makes about 100ml
(3½ fl. oz)

50–75 g (1¾–2¾ oz) scented rose petals; use pink or red petals if you want a pink syrup or jelly

1.5 litres (3¼ pints) water

For rose syrup:

Makes about 1.8 litres
(2¾ pints)

liquid left from making rose water

about 1.2 kg (2 lb 12 oz) sugar

For rose jelly:

Makes about 1.6 litres
(2½ pints) or four 450 g (1 lb) jars)

liquid left from making rose water

about 1.2 kg (2 lb 12 oz) preserving sugar (with pectin)

100 ml (3½ fl. oz) lemon juice, strained (from about 3 lemons)

To make rose syrup:

1.

Weigh the strained water into a pan and add the same weight of sugar. Heat gently, stirring until dissolved. Increase the heat, simmer for a couple of minutes, then remove from the heat and leave to cool.

2.

Decant into bottles and store in the fridge for a couple of weeks. You can freeze it if you want to keep it for longer.

Our favourite way to serve this rose syrup is as a refreshing summer cordial. To make the cordial, put 2 large sweet geranium leaves (or a handful of mint leaves) in the bottom of a large jug (pitcher) and crush lightly with the handle of a wooden spoon. Add 200 ml (7 fl. oz) rose syrup, the juice of 1 lemon and 800 ml (1½ pints) still or sparkling water. Stir well and top up with ice cubes.

THE EDIBLE FLOWER

To make rose jelly:

1.
Sterilize jam jars and lids following the method on pages 179–81. The quantities given here should make about 1.6 litres (2½ pints) of jelly, but it's always better to prepare a few extra jars. Put a small plate in the freezer, to help you test the jelly's set later.

2.
Weigh the strained water into a large pan (use a preserving pan if you have one). Weigh out the same amount of preserving sugar into a bowl. Add the lemon juice to the water in the pan and bring to the boil. Reduce the heat, add the sugar and stir well to dissolve. Once the sugar has dissolved, increase the heat and bubble vigorously for about 15 minutes, or until the temperature reaches 105°C/220°F on a jam thermometer.

3.
After 15 minutes, remove from the heat and put a teaspoon of jelly on the cold plate. Put it back in the freezer for a couple of minutes and then gently push your finger into the cold jelly. If the jelly wrinkles, it is set. If not, put the pan of jelly back on the heat for another 3 minutes and repeat the wrinkle test.

4.
Pour the jelly into the warm sterilized jars and screw on the sterilized lids. Leave to set for a further 24 hours before using. This is delicious used to sandwich together the German Biscuits with Daisies (see page 164), or on toast, on scones (biscuits) with cream, with cheese (particularly goat's cheese), to glaze tarts, such as the Blackberry and Sweet Geranium Tart (see page 288), or in marinades for lamb or pork.

Use other edible flowers to make jellies in a similar way. Elderflower, lilac and German chamomile work particularly well.

SPICED CHICKEN B'STILLA TRIANGLES

I have very happy memories of being on the roof of the Dar Les Cigognes hotel in Marrakech, eating b'stilla that we'd been taught to make by the wonderful female cooks there. Traditionally a round pie, it's so rich and sweet with egg, almonds and spices that it works well as a snack or canape. This spice mix recipe will make quite a lot more than you need. Halve the quantities, or keep it in a sealed container – it will stay fresh for a few months. Use it in marinades for lamb, chicken or root vegetables, add a teaspoon to couscous, or use it in the Courgette Flowers Stuffed with Bulgar Wheat, Green Olives and Apricots (see page 98).

Ras el hanout is a North African spice mix that is used in tagines, marinades, and chicken or pigeon b'stilla, the sweet and savoury filo pies that are the inspiration for this recipe. Ras el hanout roughly translates from Arabic as 'top of the shop', meaning the best of everything. There isn't a universally agreed recipe; instead, home cooks or spice merchants have their own closely guarded recipes, some containing more than 30 different spices. Mixes often include dried rose petals and lavender, both of which are used widely in North African cuisine. This is my version, which is warming and floral with a little freshness from the fennel.

Makes 40 triangles

For the saffron yoghurt dip:

a pinch of saffron

1 tbsp boiling water

1 small garlic clove, crushed to a paste or finely grated

a couple of drops of rose water

200 ml (7 fl. oz) Greek (strained plain) yoghurt

For the spice mix:

2 tbsp coriander seeds

2 tbsp cumin seeds

1 tbsp black peppercorns

2 tsp fennel seeds

10 allspice berries (or ½ tsp ground allspice)

4 tbsp dried rose petals

2 tsp dried lavender

2 tsp ground cinnamon

2 tsp ground ginger

1 tsp ground turmeric

1.

Put the saffron in a small bowl, pour over the boiling water and set aside. The longer it infuses (steeps), the better.

2.

Now make the spice mix. Put the coriander seeds, cumin seeds, peppercorns, fennel seeds and allspice berries in a frying pan (skillet) over a medium heat and toast for a couple of minutes, until fragrant. Transfer to a spice grinder or mortar and pestle and add the rose petals and lavender. Grind to a fine powder and then stir in the cinnamon, ginger and turmeric.

THE EDIBLE FLOWER

3.

Now make the filling. Heat the oil in a heavy pot with a lid, over a high heat. Sprinkle ½ tsp salt over the chicken, then add the meat to the pot and brown on all sides. Remove from the pot and set aside. Reduce the heat and add the chopped onion and another ½ tsp salt. Fry for 10 minutes, until soft and turning golden. Add the garlic and 2 tbsp of the spice mix and cook for another minute, stirring frequently.

4.

Return the chicken to the pot, pour over the hot stock and bring to a simmer. Reduce the heat, cover and cook for 25 minutes. Remove the chicken, discard the bones and finely chop the chicken, skin and all.

5.

Increase the heat and reduce the remaining liquid in the pot until there is only about 150 ml (5 fl. oz) left. Reduce the heat, add the eggs and cook for a couple of minutes, stirring constantly. The mixture will resemble runny scrambled eggs. Remove from the heat and stir in the chicken, almonds, honey, rose water and parsley. Taste and add more salt if necessary.

6.

Preheat the oven to 200°C/400°F/Gas 6 and line two large baking sheets with baking parchment or a silicone sheet.

7.

Cut the filo into 40 strips measuring approximately 6 × 25 cm (2½ × 9¾ in). Brush with melted butter. Put 1 heaped tsp of the chicken mixture at one end of a strip and fold over a triangle of pastry to encase the filling. Keep folding in triangles until you run out of pastry and the filling is completely enclosed. Brush the triangle with butter, sprinkle with nigella seeds and put on the baking sheet. Repeat for the other pastry strips. Bake for 30 minutes, until the pastry is golden brown and crispy.

8.

Meanwhile, add the saffron and soaking water, the garlic, rose water and a pinch of salt to the yoghurt and mix well. Serve the crispy parcels with the saffron yoghurt for dipping.

The parcels can be frozen before baking and kept until needed. Freeze on the baking sheet, then put in sealed bags or boxes once frozen, to avoid them sticking together. Cook from frozen, for about 10 minutes longer.

For the filling:

2 tbsp olive oil

500 g (1 lb 2 oz) chicken thighs (on the bone)

1 onion, finely chopped

2 garlic cloves, finely chopped

350 ml (12 fl. oz) hot chicken or vegetable stock (broth)

3 eggs, lightly beaten

75 g (2¾ oz) ground almonds

1 tbsp honey

1 tsp rose water

20 g (¾ oz) flat-leaf parsley, finely chopped

1 packet filo pastry (about 220 g/7½ oz)

100 g (3½ oz) butter, melted

nigella seeds, for sprinkling

salt

ROSE & CARDAMOM PAVLOVA WITH SUMMER BERRIES

Pavlovas are sometimes seen as retro, but they remain one of our most requested puddings for weddings. Raspberries and strawberries are delicious with rose, but because this recipe uses dried rose petals, you could make it in winter too, perhaps topping it with roasted rhubarb or poached pears. It's important to use dried rose petals because fresh petals will make the sugar damp, which could affect the texture of the meringue. The petals may turn the meringue a rather alarming blue, but don't worry – it will revert to a creamy colour on baking.

Serves 10

400 g (14 oz) caster (superfine) sugar

8 tbsp dried rose petals, plus a few extra to decorate

6 large egg whites (about 240 g/9 oz total weight)

2 tsp cornflour (cornstarch)

1 tsp white wine vinegar

seeds from 10 cardamom pods, finely ground

500 g (1 lb 2 oz) mixed strawberries and raspberries

400 ml (14 fl. oz) double (heavy) cream

a handful of dried or fresh rose petals and a few tiny mint leaves, to decorate

1.

First, make the rose sugar. Put the sugar and rose petals in a food processor and pulse until combined and finely ground.

2.

Preheat the oven to 180°C/350°F/Gas 4. Put 375 g (13 oz) of the rose sugar in a heatproof bowl in the oven for 15 minutes. Heating the sugar helps it to dissolve more easily into the egg whites, ensuring a smoother meringue. Draw a circle 25 cm (10 in) in diameter on a sheet of baking parchment, to use as a guide for the pavlova. Turn over the baking parchment (you should still be able to see the circle) and use it to line a large baking sheet.

3.

Using a stand mixer or hand-held electric mixer, whisk the egg whites until they form stiff peaks. Add the warmed sugar a tablespoon at a time, until all the sugar is incorporated and the meringue mixture is stiff and shiny. Finally, sprinkle with the cornflour (cornstarch), vinegar and ground cardamom and briefly mix again until incorporated.

4.

Spread the meringue out on the baking parchment using the circle you have drawn as a guide. Use a palette knife or spatula to smooth out the sides and top, although it doesn't have to be too neat. I like to make the edge of the circle a little higher than the middle, like a nest, so the filling sits inside the meringue.

5.

Put the pavlova in the oven and immediately turn the temperature down to 150°C/300°F/Gas 2. Bake for an hour. Turn off the oven, open the oven door slightly and allow the meringue to cool completely in the oven. You can even leave it in overnight. This is to reduce cracking, but don't worry if you still get some cracks – it just adds to the rustic beauty of the dish.

6.

While the pavlova is cooling, prepare the berries. Hull the strawberries and chop in half if they are small or quarters if they are large. Put all the berries in a bowl and add the remaining rose sugar. Mix well and leave to macerate for at least 15 minutes before using. The raspberries will break down a bit.

7.

Now assemble the pavlova. Gently remove the meringue from the parchment to a large platter. Whip the cream to soft peaks and spread it over the top, leaving a gap around the edge so that you can still see some meringue. Pile the berries on top of the cream and decorate with a few dried or fresh rose petals and a few tiny mint leaves. Serve immediately, or at least within 2 hours.

CHOCOLATE & ROSE AMARETTI

Chocolate and rose are delicious together, and these little cookies can be made out of season, perhaps as Christmas gifts, because they are flavoured with dried rose petals and rose water. They also work beautifully with lavender – just replace the dried rose petals with 2 tsp fresh or dried lavender.

1.

Preheat the oven to 170°C/325°F/Gas 3 Line two large baking sheets with baking parchment or silicone sheets and lightly oil the paper or silicone.

2.

Put the caster (superfine) sugar and rose petals into a food processor and whizz for a few seconds, until there are no large pieces of rose petal remaining. Transfer to a bowl, add the almonds and cocoa powder, and stir to mix.

3.

In a large bowl, whisk the egg whites to stiff peaks using a stand mixer or hand-held electric mixer. Fold in the sugar and almond mixture and then stir in the liqueur and rose water.

4.

Put the sugar and icing (confectioner's) sugar into two separate shallow bowls. Roll the cookie mixture into walnut-sized balls and roll each first in the sugar and then in the icing sugar. Put the cookies on the baking sheet about 2 cm (1 in) apart, as they will expand as they cook.

5.

Bake for 15–20 minutes, depending on how squishy you like them in the middle. The longer time will result in a crisper cookie. Cool completely on a wire rack before serving.

Makes 28–30 amaretti

a little sunflower oil (or another flavourless oil), for greasing

250 g (9 oz) caster (superfine) sugar

5 tbsp dried rose petals

200 g (7 oz) ground almonds

50 g (1¾ oz) cocoa (unsweetened chocolate) powder, sifted

3 large egg whites (about 120 g/4½ oz total weight)

1 tbsp amaretto (or use elderflower liqueur; see recipe on page 256)

1 tsp rose water

50 g (1¾ oz) sugar

50 g (1¾ oz) icing (confectioner's) sugar, sifted

ELDER

Sambucus nigra

Deciduous tree

Height up
to 6 m (20 ft)

Spread up
to 5 m (16½ ft)

Full sun, alkaline
or neutral soil

Plant in early winter
or early spring

Harvest flowers
in late spring

Why we grow it – Here in Northern Ireland, elder seems to appear everywhere, marking the start of summer and cordial-making season. The scent is unmistakable, both floral and musky. You can forage for elder (see page 216), but it's also a lovely addition to a large garden. Make sure you leave plenty of flower heads so that you can collect the elderberries later. They are a brilliant addition to jellies or ketchups, and make wonderful vinegar.

WARNING: Elderflowers and elderberries are edible after cooking, but all other parts of this plant are toxic and should not be eaten. Do not eat the stems or berries raw, and only eat the raw flowers in moderation.

How to propagate – Buy bare-root or container-grown plants and plant out in winter. Technically, you can plant container-grown plants at any time of year, but I would always recommend planting in winter when the plant is dormant. Alternatively, take semi-ripe cuttings in summer from new growth, or take hardwood cuttings in autumn (see page 294).

How to grow – Elder likes a sunny site and is generally unfussy about soil, although it particularly loves chalk. It has a tendency to grow with a rather upright habit, sending up lots of long, almost vertical branches. It will grow fast and soon dominate a small garden if you don't cut back all the branches in autumn, to control the overall height. Also prune out some of the central branches when it gets crowded, and prune some of the outer branches

to an outward-facing bud, to encourage the shrub into a more attractive shape.

American Elder (*Sambucus canadensis*) is a species of elder that is native to America and Canada. It has a much longer flowering period than the UK native and tastes a little different, but the flowers (and berries) can be used in the same way.

How to harvest and prep – Elderflowers are at their most fragrant when the little flowers are just opening, so I look for heads where about three-quarters of the flowers are open but a few little buds remain closed. Avoid any with browning or discoloured flowers. It is a good idea to pick them on a dry day. Harvest whole heads of flowers by hand or with secateurs, then shake them well to get rid of insects and excess pollen. Elderflower leaves and stalks are toxic, so remove all the leaves and as much of the stalk as possible (the little bit of stalk holding the flowers together is fine).

FLOWERS *in late spring.*

DO *make the most of the short flowering season.*

DON'T *be tempted to pick all the flowers. Leave some to develop into elderberries (for you and the birds).*

TASTES *delightful, with musky floral notes and a hint of pineapple.*

THE EDIBLE FLOWER

ELDER

ELDERFLOWER
FRITTER SALAD
WITH BLUE CHEESE
& HONEY

An early summer treat, elderflower fritters are more traditionally served as a dessert, but I love the way the musky flavour complements the peppery leaves and sharp blue cheese in this dish. We always incorporate elderflower into the menus for our Summer Solstice Supper Club. One year we served this salad as an appetizer and it was a big hit with our guests, many of whom hadn't tried elderflower in a savoury dish before.

**Serves 4
as an appetizer,
6 as a side dish**

8 large elderflower heads, shaken to remove any insects

¼ red onion, finely sliced

50 g (1¾ oz) plain (all-purpose) flour

50 g (1¾ oz) cornflour (cornstarch)

¼ tsp salt

100–120 ml (3½–4½ fl. oz) cold sparkling water

sunflower or vegetable oil, for frying

50 g (1¾ oz) peppery salad leaves, such as rocket (arugula), watercress or mustard leaves

150 g (5½ oz) cooked beetroot (beet) (use pre-cooked or roast your own; see instructions on pages 121–23), cubed

50 g (1¾ oz) Stilton-style blue cheese (we use Young Buck, an Irish blue)

2 tsp honey

a pinch of mild chilli flakes, such as Aleppo

a few dark cornflower petals, to garnish (optional)

1.

Break the elderflower umbels into bite-size pieces and remove almost all of the stem, leaving just a tiny bit holding the sprigs together.

2.

Put all the dressing ingredients in a jar, tighten the lid and shake well to combine. Put the red onion in a small bowl and add 1 tbsp dressing. The onion will macerate in the dressing, resulting in a milder taste.

3.

Combine the flour, cornflour and salt in a mixing bowl. Pour in the sparkling water, stirring all the time, to make a batter that is just a little thicker than double (heavy) cream. You might not need all the water, so add it gradually.

4.

Heat oil to a depth of 5 cm (2 in) in a wok or deep pan until the oil is 180°C/350°F. If you don't have a cooking thermometer, drop a small spoonful of the batter into the oil, and if it bubbles up and browns in 15 seconds, the oil is ready.

5.

Hold a piece of elderflower at the back of the flower head and dip it into the batter, completely coating the flower. Carefully drop it into the hot oil. Fry in batches of about 8 for 30–45 seconds on each side, then lift out of the oil using a slotted spoon and drain on a baking sheet lined with paper towels. We usually put the

THE EDIBLE FLOWER

fritters in a low oven (100°C/210°F/Gas ¼) to keep warm while we fry the rest.

6.

Arrange the salad leaves on individual plates or a large platter and drizzle with a little dressing. Top with the dressed onion and beetroot, crumble over the cheese and add the elderflower fritters. Drizzle with the honey and sprinkle with the chilli flakes and the cornflower petals, if using. Serve immediately.

Variation: To make sweet elderflower fritters, add 1 tbsp caster (superfine) sugar to the batter and just a pinch of salt, then cook as above. Sprinkle the fritters with icing (confectioner's) sugar before serving. The batter can also be used to make sweet or savoury dandelion fritters, and we often make this salad in early spring, when the dandelions dot our lawn and garden edges in their hundreds.

For the dressing:

2 tbsp olive oil

1 tbsp white wine vinegar

½ tsp Dijon mustard

1 tsp honey

salt and freshly ground black pepper

THE EDIBLE FLOWER

ELDERFLOWER
& LIME SYRUP CAKE

This recipe is inspired by revani, a syrup-soaked semolina cake from the Mediterranean and Middle East. Traditional recipes often use rose water or orange-blossom water, but here fragrant elderflower is the perfect addition. I would suggest serving it with thick Greek (strained plain) yoghurt and fresh fruit, such as strawberries or stone fruit. Start making the syrup the day before, unless you have elderflower cordial ready-made.

Serves 15

For the syrup:

6 large elderflower heads, with the flowers mostly open if possible

300 ml (10 fl. oz) boiling water

350 g (12 oz) sugar

juice of 2 limes

For the cake:

3 large eggs

100 g (3½ oz) sugar

200 ml (7 fl. oz) Greek (strained plain) yoghurt, plus extra to serve

150 ml (5 fl. oz) sunflower oil, plus a little extra for greasing

1 tsp vanilla extract

zest of 2 limes

200 g (7 oz) semolina

50 g (1¾ oz) plain (all-purpose) flour

2 tsp baking powder

¼ tsp salt

icing (confectioner's) sugar and elderflowers, to garnish

1.

Start making the syrup the day before you want to serve. Shake the elderflower heads to dislodge any insects, then remove most of the stalks and put the flowers in a heatproof bowl. Pour over the boiling water, cover and leave at room temperature overnight (for about 12 hours).

2.

The next day, strain the liquid into a pan through a sieve (strainer) lined with a piece of muslin (cheesecloth) or a clean dish towel, squeezing to extract all the liquid. Discard the elderflowers. Add the sugar to the pan and heat, stirring, until it has dissolved. Bring to the boil and simmer for 5 minutes. Remove from the heat, stir in the lime juice and leave to cool. The syrup must be almost cold when you put it on the cake.

3.

When you are ready to make the cake, preheat the oven to 200°C/400°F/Gas 6. Oil a 22 × 33 cm (8½ × 13 in) cake tin (pan) and line with baking parchment.

4.

Put the eggs and sugar in a large bowl or the bowl of a stand mixer and whisk on the highest setting (or very vigorously by hand) for a couple of minutes, until pale and creamy. Add the yoghurt, oil, vanilla extract and lime zest and whisk again until completely incorporated.

5.

In a separate bowl, stir together the semolina, flour, baking powder and salt. Gently fold the semolina mixture into the wet ingredients in two batches.

6.

Pour the batter into the prepared tin and bake for 15 minutes. Turn the oven down to 180°C/350°F/Gas 4 and bake for another 10–15 minutes, or until a skewer inserted into the middle comes out clean.

7.

Leave to cool in the tin for a couple of minutes and then carefully cut the cake into 15 squares while it is still hot. Drizzle the syrup over the cake – it will seem like a lot, but this is what makes the cake so moist and delicious, so do use it all. I spoon the syrup over the cake in a couple of batches, allowing it to soak in fully before adding more.

8.

Leave the cake to cool and then refrigerate for a couple of hours to allow the flavours to meld. Serve dusted with icing (confectioner's) sugar, sprinkled with a few tiny elderflowers and with a dollop of yoghurt on the side.

ELDERFLOWER LIQUEUR

This liqueur tastes floral, with an undertone of almonds and a little spice. It is a breeze to make, even easier than cordial. If you can get hold of flowers from a pink variety, you can make a gorgeous pink liqueur; the standard white elderflower will yield a pale golden drink. You can drink it neat over ice, but it is also excellent mixed with gin, lemon juice and soda water to make a punchy Elderflower Tom Collins cocktail. Alternatively, serve it topped up with sparkling wine, with a strawberry or raspberry floating in it, for a lovely early summer aperitif.

Makes about 850 ml (1½ pints)

20 freshly picked elderflower heads

zest of 1 large lemon, in large strips

750 ml (1¼ pints) vodka

75 ml (3 fl. oz) boiling water

75 g (2¾ oz) sugar

1.

Prepare the elderflower heads (see instructions on page 246). Put them in a clean 1 litre (1¾ pint) mason jar and add the lemon zest and vodka. You may find it helpful to use a smaller jar or saucer set into the top of the mason jar to keep all the flowers submerged; this will stop them from floating to the top and discolouring, which might make the liqueur a bit brown but won't affect the flavour. Seal the jar and leave in a cool, dark place for at least 2 weeks.

2.

After a couple of weeks, taste the liquid. If the flavour isn't strong enough, leave it for another week or two. If it is strong enough, strain it through a fine sieve (strainer), then strain it again through a sieve lined with a piece of muslin (cheesecloth), a clean dish towel or even just a couple of paper towels. This will remove even the tiniest bugs and pollen.

3.

Pour the boiling water over the sugar in a jug (pitcher) and stir to dissolve. Leave to cool, then add to the liqueur. This is how sweet I like the liqueur, but you can add more or less sugar to taste. Pour the sweetened liqueur into clean bottles to store. You can drink it immediately, but I find the flavour improves after about a month. Because of the alcohol content the liqueur will keep forever.

Consider making flavoured liqueurs with other edible flowers – rose, hawthorn, magnolia and carnation all work well. See also the recipe for Dill Flower Aquavit on page 75.

HAWTHORN

Crataegus monogyna

Deciduous tree

Height and spread up
to 8 m (25 ft)

Full sun or partial shade,
well-drained soil

Plant in early winter or
early spring

Harvest flowers in spring

Why we grow it – Hawthorn is spectacular in early summer, when the hedgerows are laden with its creamy, pink-tinged blooms. It was traditionally considered very unlucky to bring it into the house, a belief that persists today. We ignore this in order to use the deliciously almondy blossoms in our cooking, but consider yourself warned! After the flowers fade in early autumn the berries (known as haws) ripen to a dark, glossy red. They are delicious in jellies and ketchups, ideally balanced with other fruit, since the flavour is quite tannic.

WARNING: Hawthorn extract is used in heart medication. If you have heart trouble or are taking heart medication, seek advice before eating hawthorn.

How to propagate – Purchase and plant bare-root trees (known as whips) in early winter or early spring. You can also dig up the seedlings that often spring up close to hawthorn hedges (assuming you have permission from the landowner). For a hedge, plant three or four whips or seedlings per metre (yard). Hawthorn can also be grown as a stand-alone tree.

Hawthorn can be grown from seed, but it is a slow process. The seeds are found inside the haws. To encourage germination, it's worth putting the haws in the fridge in a small bag of damp sand or leaf mould for two or three weeks. This period of cold, which mimics winter weather and tricks the seeds into coming out of their dormant state, is called cold stratification and encourages quicker and more successful germination.

How to grow – Little maintenance is required unless you are growing your hawthorn as a hedge, which should be trimmed every year or so.

How to harvest and prep – Use secateurs or scissors to cut off flower heads when most of the flowers are open, but before they start to discolour and brown. To use them in the kitchen, pick individual flowers off the stalks, removing as much of the stem as possible. Don't forget to leave some flower heads if you want haws to use later in the year. If you are foraging for hawthorn rather than using your own tree, be sure of your identification and follow the foraging guidelines on page 216.

FLOWERS *in late spring/early summer.*

DO *use the flowers raw, sprinkled over blanched asparagus (which is in season at the same time) or sliced tomatoes. They have a distinctive almondy flavour and look stunning on a salad.*

DON'T *forget to eat the bright green, young leaves in early spring, as a great addition to a green salad.*

TASTES *of almonds, with a hint of bitterness.*

HAWTHORN, APRICOT & CHOCOLATE BREAD-&-BUTTER PUDDING

Bread-and-butter pudding is one of Jo's childhood favourites, but here I've given it a sophisticated twist with an almondy hawthorn custard, apricots and dark chocolate. For this recipe it is worth seeking out good-quality white bread from a bakery. Mass-produced sliced bread will not soak up the custard properly.

Serves 8

50 g (1¾ oz) hawthorn blossom (ideally newly opened flowers)

650 ml (22 fl. oz) whole (full-cream) milk

4 large eggs

100 g (3½ oz) caster (superfine) sugar

75 g (2¾ oz) butter, melted, plus extra butter for greasing

100 g (3½ oz) dried apricots, coarsely chopped

100 g (3½ oz) 70% dark chocolate or chocolate drops, coarsely chopped

8 thin slices good-quality white bread (350–400 g/12–14 oz total weight)

2 tbsp Demerara sugar

pouring cream, to serve

1.

Pick the flowers off the hawthorn into a large pan. It's fine if there are little stalks left on the flowers, but you don't want any woody bits or leaves. Add the milk and slowly bring to a simmer over a low heat; this should take about 15 minutes. Once the milk is just simmering, remove from the heat and leave to steep for at least half an hour and up to 2 hours.

2.

Meanwhile, butter an ovenproof dish measuring about 22 × 22 × 5 cm (9 × 9 × 2 in).

3.

Line a sieve (strainer) with a piece of muslin (cheesecloth) or a clean dish towel and strain the milk into a large measuring jug (pitcher). Squeeze the muslin to make sure you have extracted all the infused milk, then discard the hawthorn.

4.

Whisk the eggs and sugar in a large mixing bowl for a minute, until combined, then pour on the infused milk, whisking constantly. Transfer the mixture into the measuring jug so that you can easily pour it over the pudding.

5.

Now assemble the pudding. Brush one side of each slice of bread with the melted butter. Cut a few slices into neat triangles and set these aside for the top layer of the pudding. Use the remaining pieces of bread to line the bottom of the prepared dish, butter side up. Sprinkle with half the apricots and chocolate. Add another layer of buttered bread, the rest of the apricots and chocolate, then finally arrange the buttered triangles in a neat pattern on top.

6.

Pour over the hawthorn custard, lightly pushing down the bread to soak into the custard. If it seems as though all the custard won't fit, leave it to soak in for a minute or two and you should be able to add more. Sprinkle the Demerara sugar over the top. Leave to rest for about an hour, so the bread melds with the custard.

7.

About 15 minutes before you want to bake the pudding, preheat the oven to 170°C/325°F/Gas 3. Bake for 30–35 minutes, until the custard is set and the pudding is golden brown on top. Serve warm, with a drizzle of cream for extra decadence.

LILAC

Syringa vulgaris

Shrub or tree

Height and spread up
to 5 m (16 ft)

Full sun, well-drained
alkaline or neutral soil

Separate suckers in spring

Harvest flowers
in early summer

Why we grow it – For some reason, lilac is rather unfashionable, often found commonly in older gardens but rarely introduced into new ones. Perhaps the short flowering season is the reason. But the smell of its flowers is truly marvellous, and it's a low–maintenance shrub that is very simple to grow and wonderful as a cut flower and edible.

How to propagate – You can buy lilac plants in pots or take softwood cuttings from a neighbour or friend's tree, but my favourite method is to take suckers or shoots from around the base of a tree in spring. Lilac trees grown from suckers will flower much more quickly than those grown from cuttings.

Find a friend's lilac tree that you like. Remember that the new plant will be a clone of the parent, so the flower colour and other characteristics will be the same. Springing up from the soil around the base of the plant will be various shoots. Find one that is far enough away from the main tree that you can put a spade between the shoot and the tree. Slice down firmly to detach the shoot, ideally leaving plenty of roots on the shoot. Plant it immediately in a pot so that it can get over the shock of the detachment, then plant it in your chosen location a month or two, or even a whole season, later.

How to grow – Lilacs are quite unfussy, but they do thrive in chalky soil. More importantly, it should be well drained. My soil is slightly acidic, so I throw a handful of lime around the base of my lilac each winter. For lilac to flower well, it must be in a sunny spot. I would also recommend annual pruning during the summer, after flowering. It's good to prune out older wood from low down. Lilacs produce flowers on last year's wood, so heavy winter pruning means no flowers for a season or two. However, if you find your flower panicles are getting smaller each year, pruning harder in summer or winter should solve the problem in the long term.

How to harvest and prep – Cut off the bunches of flowers with secateurs.

FLOWERS *in early summer.*

DO *remember to prune after flowering.*

DON'T *bother to deadhead, unless for aesthetic reasons.*

TASTES *less intense than it smells.*

THE EDIBLE FLOWER

LILAC
PANNA COTTA WITH
STRAWBERRIES

The smell of lilac on a warm May day is so fiercely lovely it is almost overpowering. However, extracting that scent into food is an art. I've had most success with slowly infusing the blossom into cream, and with making lilac sugar, and have found that it's best to use the flowers immediately after harvesting. This recipe can be adapted for any other sweetly scented edible flower – try it with elderflower, lavender, hawthorn blossom, rose petals or sweet geranium leaves.

If you are nervous about turning out the panna cotta, make it in pretty individual dishes.

Serves 6

60 g (2¼ oz) lilac flowers (about 6 large flower heads)

sunflower oil, for greasing

600 ml (20 fl. oz) double (heavy) cream

100 ml (3½ fl. oz) whole (full-cream) milk

2½ sheets of gelatine

60 g (2¼ oz) caster (superfine) sugar

200 g (7 oz) strawberries

1 tbsp lilac sugar (see recipe on page 269) or plain caster sugar

1.

Pick the individual flowers off the lilac panicles, removing as much green stalk as you possibly can and reserving a few flowers for the garnish.

2.

Put the flowers, cream and milk in a large pan over a low heat and bring to a simmer. Remove from the heat and leave to cool, then refrigerate overnight (or for at least 8 hours) to infuse (steep).

3.

Strain the cream through a sieve (strainer) lined with a piece of muslin (cheesecloth) or a dish towel, into a clean pan. Squeeze the cloth to extract as much liquid and flavour as possible.

4.

Put the gelatine in a small bowl of cold water to soak for 5 minutes. Grease six 150 ml (5 fl. oz) dariole moulds very lightly with sunflower oil.

5.

Heat the cream over a medium heat, add the sugar and stir to dissolve. Bring to a simmer and remove from the heat. Squeeze the gelatine well to remove any excess water, then add it to the hot cream and stir well until completely dissolved.

6.

Pour the cream into the prepared moulds and leave to cool, then put in the fridge to set for at least 5 hours or preferably overnight.

7.

About half an hour before serving, hull and quarter the strawberries and mix with the 1 tbsp sugar. Set aside to macerate.

8.

To turn out the panna cottas, dip the bottom of each mould into a bowl of boiling water for a couple of seconds and invert it on to a serving plate. While holding it against the plate, give it a couple of firm shakes. The panna cotta should plop onto the plate; if it doesn't, I find carefully running a sharp knife around the edge of the mould helps to release the seal.

9.

Serve with the macerated strawberries and a few lilac flowers to garnish. Lavender Shortbread (see page 176) is a delicious accompaniment, especially if you make it with lilac sugar instead of lavender.

LILAC SUGAR

This method for making floral sugar is perfect for lilacs, which do not keep their fragrance when dried. It is a slower method, allowing the sugar to absorb the volatile oils in the lilac blossoms.

This method can be used with other highly scented flowers such as elderflowers, roses, violets and lavender. With lavender, just five stalks will be enough to flavour a small jar of sugar.

1.

Put a 1 cm (½ in) layer of sugar in the bottom of a 500 g (1 lb 2 oz) mason jar, then a layer of lilac flowers followed by another layer of sugar. Repeat until you have filled the jar and used all the flowers; be sure to finish with a layer of sugar. Leave the jar out on your work surface and shake it every day for a week. The shaking helps to coat the lilac in the sugar and stops the sugar from clumping too much from the moisture in the lilacs.

2.

After a week, open the jar and sift the sugar, ideally through a sieve (strainer) with quite large mesh, to remove all the brown bits of lilac.

3.

Because of the moisture in the lilacs, I find it very hard to grind the sugar because it clumps. It is best to dry it out first. Preheat the oven to 50°C/120°F/Gas ¼. Spread the sugar on a baking sheet lined with baking parchment or a silicone mat and cook in the oven for 15 minutes. (You can also simply leave the baking sheet in a warm place for a couple of hours.) Leave to cool, then put the sugar in a food processor or exceptionally clean spice/coffee grinder and whizz for a few seconds until it is the consistency of caster (superfine) sugar and perfect for sprinkling.

Makes 350 g (12 oz)

300 g (10½ oz) sugar

50 g (1¾ oz) freshly picked lilac petals, green stalks removed

RICOTTA DOUGHNUTS WITH LILAC & LEMON

This is an adaptable recipe and can be made with all sorts of floral sugar – try it with lavender or sweet geranium sugar. I like to think of it as a special brunch dish, rather than a dessert, because you really have to eat the doughnuts immediately and I don't want to start deep-frying late in the evening after hosting a dinner party. If you have already made the sugar, this is quick to make, hardly more complicated than making pancakes. You can make it even more special by adding lemon curd for dipping.

Makes about 20 small doughnuts

100 g (3½ oz) plain (all-purpose) flour

1 tsp baking powder

5 tbsp Lilac Sugar (see page 267)

250 g (9 oz) drained full-fat ricotta cheese

2 large eggs

zest of 1 small lemon

sunflower oil, for frying

salt

1.

Stir together the flour, baking powder, 2 tbsp of the sugar and a pinch of salt in a mixing bowl until any clumps are broken up and all the ingredients are evenly distributed.

2.

In a separate large bowl, beat the ricotta, eggs and lemon zest with a wooden spoon until combined. Add the dry ingredients and fold together until you have a smooth, thick batter.

3.

Pour oil to a depth of at least 6 cm (2½ in) into a wide, deep pan or deep-fryer and heat to 180°C/350°F. If you don't have a cooking thermometer, you can check the oil is ready by putting the end of a wooden spoon or wooden chopstick into the oil. If bubbles form and slowly but steadily rise to the surface, the oil is hot enough. Use two teaspoons to carefully drop smooth, oval-shaped dollops of the batter into the hot oil. Fry in batches of about 8, for about 3 minutes, turning frequently with a slotted spoon, until golden and crispy.

4.

Remove the cooked doughnuts from the oil with the slotted spoon, drain on paper towels, and roll to coat in the remaining lilac sugar while still warm. Put them in a low oven to keep warm while you fry the rest, if you like. Serve immediately.

SAUCER MAGNOLIA

Magnolia × soulangeana

Large deciduous tree

Height and spread up to 8 m (25 ft)

Plant in early winter or early spring

Harvest flowers in early spring

Why we grow it – These majestic, ancient trees are thought to look similar to the very first flowering plants on Earth. The petals taste delicious: gingery with notes of cardamom, citrus and black pepper, although this varies by species. The saucer magnolia is a tasty and popular cultivar. It's easier to grow than some and is deciduous, giving you the delight of bare branches laden with large flowers each spring before the leaves unfurl.

How to propagate – It is possible to grow magnolia trees from seed or from softwood or semi-ripe cuttings, but given that it is relatively slow-growing, most people choose to purchase a tree from a nursery.

How to grow – The saucer magnolia is one of the easier magnolias to grow. Magnolias are famous for their need for acidic soil and very sheltered sites, but *Magnolia × soulangeana* is slightly more forgiving on both counts. Finding the right spot is probably the most challenging part of growing a saucer magnolia. Over the decades it will grow into a large, spreading tree, so it's not for every garden.

How to harvest – Break off whole flowers when they are still young or in bud. We generally use just the petals, although the pineapple-shaped centre of the flower (which holds the stamen and stigma) is also edible.

FLOWERS *in early spring.*

DO *use the flowers to flavour puddings, and pickle the petals or whole buds to preserve.*

DON'T *steal flowers. If you don't have your own tree, ask permission from the owner before harvesting.*

TASTE *ranges from mild to strong ginger, sometimes with a hint of cardamom or citrus. Some varieties are bitter, so do taste before using.*

PICKLED MAGNOLIA

Pickled magnolia petals are a revelation. The sweet pickle balances out any bitterness in the flowers and allows their gingery magnificence to shine through. They taste like the Japanese pickled ginger that we often associate with eating sushi, albeit with a silkier texture. Serve with sushi, steak or other grilled meats, chopped up in stir-fries and salads, or – our favourite – with Aubergine Katsu Curry (see page 278). Once you have finished eating the petals, use the remaining ginger-scented vinegar in salad dressings or to pickle something else, such as radishes.

Makes one 350–400 ml (12–14 fl. oz) jar

200 ml (7 fl. oz) rice vinegar

75 g (2¾ oz) sugar

1 tsp salt

several fresh magnolia flowers (enough for the petals to fill the jar when tightly packed)

1.

Heat the vinegar, sugar and salt gently in a small pan and stir to dissolve the sugar. Increase the heat and bring to a simmer.

2.

Meanwhile, pluck the petals off the magnolia flowers, shaking out any bugs and removing any brown bits. Discard the central pineapple-shaped bit and any sepals (the bit that would have originally covered the bud), which often have a furry texture. Pack the petals into a clean 350–400 ml (12–14 fl. oz) jar.

3.

As soon as the vinegar starts simmering, remove it from the heat. Leave to cool for a minute or two, so it doesn't crack the jar, and pour it over the petals in the jar. The liquid should come right to the top. Leave to cool, then refrigerate for at least 24 hours before eating. The petals will turn beigey-brown, but this is absolutely fine; unfortunately they don't keep their colour, but they will still taste delicious.

AUBERGINE KATSU CURRY WITH PICKLED MAGNOLIA

When I first tasted pickled magnolia, this is what I imagined eating it with. Ginger and aubergine are a match made in heaven, and the sharpness of the pickle cuts through the rich sauce and fried aubergine (eggplant). You can easily make this dish vegan if you replace the egg with soya milk thickened with a little cornflour (cornstarch). This curry is also great with Pickled Kohlrabi, Cucumber and Borage Salad (see page 37).

Serves 4

For the sauce:

1 tbsp sunflower oil

1 large carrot, chopped

1 large onion, chopped

3 garlic cloves, finely chopped or grated

3 cm (1¼ in) piece fresh ginger, finely chopped or grated

1½ tsp curry powder

½ tsp turmeric

1 tbsp soy sauce

2 tsp soft brown sugar

200 ml (7 fl. oz) thick coconut milk

200 ml (7 fl. oz) water

1.

Slice the aubergine into rounds about 1.5 cm (¾ in) thick, aiming for about 12 slices. Layer them in a colander over a plate or bowl and sprinkle with about 1 tsp salt, coating both sides of the slices. Put a plate on top to weigh the aubergine down and help to draw out the moisture. Leave for half an hour.

2.

Now make the curry sauce. Heat the oil in a medium pan, add the carrot and onion with a pinch of salt and cook with the lid on for 10 minutes, until starting to soften. Add the garlic, ginger, curry powder and turmeric, and cook uncovered for a couple more minutes. Add the soy sauce, sugar, coconut milk and water, bring to a simmer and cook uncovered for about 10 minutes, or until the carrots and onions are completely soft. Using a hand-held blender or an ordinary blender, blend the sauce until smooth.

3.

Heat oil to 180°C/350°F in a wok or deep-fryer. Meanwhile, put the flour, egg and panko breadcrumbs in three separate shallow bowls and season the flour with salt and pepper. If you don't have a cooking thermometer, you can check the oil is ready by putting the end of a wooden spoon or wooden chopstick into the oil. If bubbles form and slowly but steadily rise to the surface, the oil is hot enough. However, if it bubbles very vigorously it may be too hot, so turn off the heat and leave to cool a little before trying again. You don't want the oil to be too hot, because the aubergine must cook through before the outside gets too brown.

4.

Wipe any excess moisture and salt off the aubergine slices and then dip them in the flour, followed by the beaten egg and finally the breadcrumbs, aiming to cover each slice completely with each layer. Put about 5 aubergine slices carefully into the hot oil at a time; don't crowd the pan or the oil will cool too much for successful cooking. Fry for about 3 minutes on each side, until golden and crispy on the outside and soft in the middle. Drain on a baking sheet lined with paper towels and keep warm in a low oven while you cook the rest.

5.

Reheat the curry sauce in a pan and serve the crispy aubergine on top of the sauce. Serve with steamed jasmine rice, fresh coriander (cilantro), pickled magnolia and slices of red chilli.

For the aubergine katsu:

1 large aubergine (eggplant) (or 2 small ones)

sunflower oil, for deep-frying

50 g (1¾ oz) plain (all-purpose) flour

1 large egg, beaten

150 g (5½ oz) panko breadcrumbs

salt and freshly ground black pepper

To serve:

steamed jasmine rice

a small bunch of coriander (cilantro) leaves

Pickled Magnolia (see page 277)

1 red chilli, sliced

MAGNOLIA RICE PUDDING WITH RHUBARB COMPOTE

Magnolia's strongly gingery, cardamom flavour lends itself beautifully to a lighter, kheer-style rice pudding with rhubarb. Kheer is an Indian milk pudding often flavoured with cardamom, ginger, rose, saffron or dried fruit and made with basmati instead of pudding rice. This is the perfect make-ahead dessert for a springtime dinner. The flavour of magnolia petals varies, so do check how strong yours are — a little bitterness is fine, as it will be balanced out with the other ingredients.

Forced rhubarb is perfect for this dish because it adds a gorgeous pink colour. If you use regular rhubarb, add a couple of dried hibiscus flowers when cooking to enhance the colour.

Serves 6

1 litre (1¾ pints) whole (full-cream) milk

50 large, fresh magnolia petals, roughly chopped

100 g (3½ oz) basmati rice

75 g (2¾ oz) caster (superfine) sugar

250 ml (8½ fl. oz) double (heavy) cream, softly whipped

salt

2 tsp dark brown sugar, to serve

For the rhubarb compote:

150 g (5½ oz) sugar

400 g (14 oz) forced rhubarb

10 large magnolia petals, sliced into thin strips

1.

Put the milk and magnolia petals in a large pan and slowly bring to a simmer over a medium-low heat. Remove from the heat and leave to steep for at least half an hour or up to 2 hours.

2.

Meanwhile, make the rhubarb compote. Pour 225 ml (7 fl. oz) boiling water over the sugar in a heatproof jug (pitcher) or bowl and stir to dissolve. Leave to cool.

3.

Trim the rhubarb and cut into 3–4 cm (1½ in) lengths. If some stems are very thick, cut them a little shorter, to ensure all the pieces cook evenly. Put them in the pan, ideally in one layer, but don't worry too much if a few bits are doubled up. They will shrink as they cook, and will be in a single layer by the end. Add the sliced magnolia petals on top and pour over the cooled syrup — it should come most of the way up the rhubarb.

4.

Bring the pan to a simmer with the lid on. Keep an eye on it, and when it starts to simmer, cook for just 1 minute more, then remove from the heat. Keep the lid on so that the rhubarb finishes cooking in the residual heat.

5.

Rinse the rice in a sieve (strainer) under cold running water until the water runs clear. Put it in a bowl, cover with cold water and leave to soak for 30 minutes.

6.

Once the milk has infused, strain through a fine sieve or clean piece of muslin (cheesecloth) to remove the magnolia petals. Return the milk to the clean pan, bring to a simmer and add the rice.

7.

Simmer for about 25 minutes, stirring frequently. You will need to stir more as it thickens. Towards the end of the cooking time, add the caster sugar and a pinch of salt and stir to dissolve. Cook for a few minutes more, until the pudding reaches the consistency of a loose porridge (oatmeal) and when most of the milk has been absorbed, then remove from the heat. Leave to cool a little; it will thicken more as it does so.

8.

Divide the cooked rhubarb between 6 serving glasses, but don't add much of the poaching liquid. Carefully dollop the rice pudding on top of the rhubarb, then refrigerate for a couple of hours. Just before serving, spoon the cream on top and sprinkle with a little brown sugar.

TIP: After removing the rhubarb from the poaching liquid, strain the liquid and store in a bottle in the fridge. Add it to drinks, drizzle it over ice cream or porridge (oatmeal), or use it to poach more rhubarb.

SWEET GERANIUM

Pelargonium graveolens

Tender perennial

Height up
to 1.2 m (4 ft)

Spread up
to 1 m (3 ft)

Full sun, well-drained soil

Take softwood
cuttings all year round

Harvest flowers
in summer and autumn

Why we grow it – We first came across sweet geranium when Erin was studying at Ballymaloe Cookery School, where it is used liberally to flavour desserts, cakes and preserves.
It is a delightful, but tender shrub with deeply lobed, highly fragrant, hairy leaves and small pink flowers. Its leaves bring a magical lemony-rose aroma to cakes, compotes, crumbles and puddings.

How to propagate – Ideally, take softwood cuttings in early summer, before flowering – but in fact cuttings are successful at almost any time of year.

How to grow – Sweet geraniums, like other pelargoniums, enjoy sunshine and warmth and can cope with dry conditions. In temperate climates they are ideal in pots, because they must be brought inside before the first frost. Cut the plant right back when you bring it in; it will tolerate hard pruning. Allow the plants to dry out almost entirely over winter by watering them very

infrequently, then water more and move the pots somewhere light as temperatures increase in spring.

How to harvest – Unlike many of the plants in this book, we recommend you mostly use the leaves of this plant, rather than the flowers! Use scissors to cut them off, or remove whole stems if your plant is getting leggy. The flowers are pretty and can be used fresh to decorate cakes, but they tend to be sparse.

FLOWERS *in summer and autumn.*

DO *store leaves in the fridge in a sealed box or bag for a couple of weeks before use (if needed). You can also freeze the leaves.*

DON'T *leave the plants outside in winter. Sweet geranium is tender and will be killed by frost.*

TASTES *of lemons and roses.*

THE EDIBLE FLOWER

SWEET GERANIUM

BLACKBERRY
& SWEET
GERANIUM TART

This is one of our most popular desserts at The Edible Flower. It is fruity and zingy, and looks like a beautiful tart without the hassle of making pastry. You can swap the blackberries for raspberries, nectarines, apricots or pears, but this is my favourite version. Sweet geranium leaves are quite robust, so do chop them very finely when making this recipe. They will add a beautiful fleck of lime green to the batter.

Serves 10

20 g (¾ oz) flaked (slivered) almonds

75 g (2¾ oz) plain (all-purpose) flour (gluten-free flour works perfectly here, too)

265 g (9½ oz) icing (confectioner's) sugar

150 g (5½ oz) ground almonds

zest of 1 lemon

3 large sweet geranium leaves, very finely chopped, plus a couple more leaves and flowers to garnish

265 g (9½ oz) egg white (from 6 or 7 eggs)

265 g (9½ oz) melted butter, plus a little extra butter for greasing

300 g (10½ oz) blackberries

2 tbsp redcurrant or rose jelly (see recipe on page 231)

1.

Preheat the oven to 200°C/400°F/Gas 6. While it is heating, spread out the flaked almonds on a baking sheet and toast in the oven for a few minutes, until just turning golden brown. Set aside.

2.

Butter a 25 cm (10 in) loose-bottomed tart tin (pan). If you are using a fluted tin, take care to grease the flutes really well, or the tart might stick.

3.

Sift the flour and icing sugar together into a bowl and stir in the ground almonds, lemon zest and geranium leaves.

4.

In a separate bowl, whisk the egg whites until just frothy. This should take about a minute.

5.

Add the egg whites and melted butter to the dry ingredients and gently fold together until really well combined. Pour the mixture into the prepared tin.

6.

Arrange the blackberries on top of the batter. I like to make concentric circles, but just sprinkle them over if you prefer.

288   THE EDIBLE FLOWER

7.

Bake for about 10 minutes, then reduce the temperature to 180°C/350°F/Gas 4 and bake for 20–25 minutes more, or until golden brown. Leave to cool in the tin.

8.

Melt the jelly in a small pan over a low heat; it will take about 15 minutes to become liquid. If it reduces too much, add a splash of water. Brush it over the top of the tart as a glaze and then sprinkle with the toasted almonds. Decorate with a couple of sweet geranium leaves and flowers.

SWEET GERANIUM SORBET

A little sweet geranium goes a long way. You need only 8 large leaves for this sorbet, but the flavour is delicious, with soft lemony undertones. When paired with the apple juice, it almost tastes of melon. Serve with sliced fruit; melon, peaches and nectarines all work beautifully for a light dessert. Alternatively, for a really fancy cocktail, half-fill a cocktail glass with sparkling wine and add 25 ml (1 fl. oz) vodka or calvados, and then a scoop of the sorbet. Top up with sparkling wine and garnish with sweet geranium leaves or flowers. Remember to start this recipe the day before you want to serve it.

Makes about 1 litre (1¾ pints), or 12 scoops

8 large sweet geranium leaves, plus a few extra leaves and flowers to garnish

350 g (12 oz) sugar

750 ml (1¼ pints) water

250 ml (8½ fl. oz) good-quality cloudy apple juice

about 3 tbsp lemon juice

1.

Put the geranium leaves, sugar and water in a pan over a medium-low heat. Stir until all the sugar is dissolved, then bring slowly to a simmer and allow to bubble gently for 2 minutes.

2.

Remove from the heat, stir in the apple juice and leave to cool. Refrigerate overnight to allow the flavours to meld.

3.

The following day, add lemon juice to taste and strain to remove the leaves and any fibres. Churn using an ice-cream maker, then put the sorbet in a container in the freezer for a couple of hours to firm up before serving.

4.

Half an hour before you are ready to serve, transfer the sorbet to the fridge, so it is scoopable. Serve garnished with tiny sweet geranium leaves or flowers.

* HOW TO *

TAKE CUTTINGS

Be warned: taking cuttings can become addictive. It's a lovely way of getting new, 'free' plants from your own or your friends' gardens. Remember that you are effectively creating a clone of the mother plant, so choose one that has the characteristics you want. Disease can be passed easily from the mother plant to the offspring (much more so than when sowing seed), so be careful to choose a specimen that is healthy and happy.

It's not possible to take cuttings of everything. For example, you can't take cuttings from annual plants; sexual reproduction through seed is the only option there. There are various different types of cutting that are characterized by the age of the material you will use. Softwood cuttings use new, young growth. Semi-ripe cuttings use slightly older growth and hardwood cuttings use growth that is almost a year old and fully hardened into proper woody material.

As a general rule, the younger the material (as with softwood cuttings), the more readily and quickly it creates new roots and successfully adapts to become a new plant. However, softwood cuttings are also much quicker to dry out and/or succumb to fungal infection. With hardwood cuttings, you'll have a higher failure rate but there is very little effort involved. They don't dry out quickly, so you don't have to create a humid environment for them.

There are sadly no general rules for what type of cutting is suitable for each plant. Some plants will successfully reproduce using all three types of cutting, and some are much more fussy. You either have to learn through trial and error, or look it up before you give it a go.

Along the stem of a plant there are nodes. These are the points where a leaf, leaves or side shoots grow from the stem. It's from these nodes that, given the right conditions (such as being buried in damp compost), roots might form. So when you're looking for good material for taking cuttings, you're looking for stems with plenty of nodes, ideally close together. If you bury more than one nodal point when taking a cutting, there is more chance of a good root system developing.

294

THE EDIBLE FLOWER

Hardwood cuttings
(late Autumn & Winter)

1.

Unlike with softwood and semi-ripe cuttings, you can make several cuttings from one branch when taking hardwood cuttings. Find an appropriate branch on the parent plant and cut it off with clean secateurs just above a node. It should be healthy and ideally have plenty of nodes, not too far apart.

2.

Cut the branch into sections. Cut with a slanted cut at the top of each cutting and a 90-degree cut at the bottom, so you know which end is which. Each section should be trimmed so that it has a nodal point at both top and bottom, and at least one nodal point between the two ends.

3.

Push the cuttings into the ground 30 cm (12 in) apart in a weed-free, sheltered spot in the garden.

4.

Lift and replant the rooted cuttings in winter, at least one full season later, into their final location. Other than making sure they don't dry out, they require very little maintenance or attention.

If you don't have space in the garden for cuttings, you can also use pots filled with an equal mix of compost and grit. I find they dry out more easily, so do keep an eye on the watering.

Softwood cuttings
(Spring & early Summer)
and semi-ripe cuttings
(late Summer & Autumn)

1.

Find a suitable mother plant, one that is healthy and happy and has the characteristic you want to reproduce (such as a particular flower colour or variegated leaves). Identify a shoot that will make a suitable cutting. It should be soft, new growth that hasn't flowered yet. Each shoot you cut off will become one cutting.

2.

Use clean secateurs to cut off the shoot just above a node. The length of cutting you are aiming for depends on the species, but about 10 cm (4 in) is a good average. More importantly, you're looking for a stem with several nodes. If you're not going to plant the cuttings immediately, store them in sealed plastic bags in the fridge.

3.

Prepare your pots and growing medium. I use a big pot with a little pot set into it to minimize the amount of compost I use (and to allow me to remove the inner pot later to check the roots). My growing medium is a mixture of compost and vermiculite. I use semi-sterile bought (peat-free, organic) compost for this, rather than my homemade compost, to cut down the risk of infection.

4.

Now prepare the cuttings. Remove all the leaves on the lower half of each cutting and most from the top half of the stem. Trim the bottom of the cutting to just below a node.

5.

Dip each cutting in hormone rooting powder and push into the growing medium, making a hole first using a chopstick or the wrong end of a pencil if the stem is very flimsy. Water well and cover loosely with a plastic bag to trap in the moisture.

6.

Leave the pots in a light, warm place, out of direct sunlight. Warmth will encourage roots to form quickly, but too hot and you risk your cuttings drying out and dying. I find a north-facing windowsill in a cool room to be ideal.

7.

Check the pots regularly, water if necessary, remove any dead cuttings and then move to a larger pot once the leaves start to grow.

INDEX

ACKNOWLEDGEMENTS

Thanks, firstly, to all our teachers – in both cooking and growing – who have taught us so well and inspired us on our journey.

Thanks to all the friends, family, customers and collaborators of The Edible Flower who have cheered us on, kept coming to our events and let us know that our business and vision is worthwhile and meaningful. To those of you who often asked when we were going to write a book – here it is!

Thanks to everyone in our lovely (but tiny) team who go above and beyond to make our events and produce brilliant and beautiful.

Thanks to Clare McQuillan who helped us find magnolia flowers when we needed them, and who is always an amazing guide to the edibility of wild flowers. And thanks to Wendy Scott who provided us with armfuls of lilacs from her own garden!

Thanks to Zara Larcombe for approaching us to write this book, to Elen Jones and Katherine Pitt for guiding us through the process, and to everyone else at Laurence King for all their stellar efforts.

Thanks to Juliet Pickering, our agent at Blake Friedmann, for making the business side of book writing as painless as possible and for answering our many silly questions. Thanks to Olia Hercules who so kindly shared her first book proposal and to Naomi Leon who gave us lots of advice on publishing and agents when we knew nothing!

Many, many thanks to Lynn Bunting (Erin's Mum) for offering to look after our twin girls all day on Mondays so we could carve out a little more time for writing this book.

And most importantly, thank you to Sharon Cosgrove, food photographer extraordinaire, who made us believe we could write this book, who is so brilliant and fun to work and who takes glorious photographs!

We'd like to acknowledge and thank the earth, both planet and soil, as our greatest teacher and collaborator – living here, learning here, on this land, over the last six years has been a privilege. We hope to continue to respond to its rhythms and delight in all that it yields.

ABOUT THE AUTHORS

Jo is an organic gardener and teacher who is passionate about encouraging others to grow their own food. She grows vegetables and edible flowers commercially, both for the catering and supper club business, and for sale to the public. She is a soil and compost fanatic and is interested in exploring various forms of sustainable food production and regenerative agriculture. Alongside growing vegetables and making compost, she loves cooking with fire, brewing beer, and spreadsheets.

Erin is a cook, teacher, recipe developer and edible flower enthusiast. She retrained at Ballymaloe Cookery School in 2015, and now spends her days developing menus and new recipes and leading a kitchen team to deliver all sorts of events and workshops. Her food is fresh, unpretentious, beautiful, vegetable-focused and inspired by the seasonal produce that Jo grows in the kitchen garden.

LAURENCE KING

First published in Great Britain in 2023
by Laurence King, an imprint of
The Orion Publishing Group Ltd
Carmelite House, 50 Victoria
Embankment, London EC4Y 0DZ

An Hachette UK Company

10 9 8 7 6 5 4 3 2 1

A CIP catalogue record for this book
is available from the British Library.

ISBN 978-0-8578-2949-8

Photography: Sharon Cosgrove
Senior Editor: Katherine Pitt
Design: Mylène Mozas & Florian Michelet

Origination by DL Imaging, UK

Printed in China by C&C Offset Printing Co. Ltd

www.laurenceking.com
www.orionbooks.co.uk

The Edible Flower disclaimer

Authors' Notes
Some of the plants in this book are edible in their
entirety, but a few have parts (leaves, stems, seeds or roots)
that are toxic. Don't assume that because the flower is
edible, other parts of the plant are too. We give warnings
about this on the appropriate pages.

None of the flowers in this book are common allergens,
but, as with all new foods, please be cautious and try
them in small quantities initially.

Notes for Cooks
As all ovens vary, cooking times and temperatures in
the recipes are for guidance. If you are using a fan oven,
reduce the temperatures stated in the recipes by about
10–20°C/50–70°F.

Teaspoons and tablespoons are level. 1 tsp = 5 ml
(0.2 fl. oz) and 1 tbsp = 15 ml (0.5 fl. oz)

Eggs are large (US extra-large). Please always use
free-range eggs.

Garlic cloves and onions are large and peeled, unless
otherwise specified. Source organic vegetables if you can.

Sugar is granulated, unless otherwise stated.
Salt is table salt unless sea salt is specified.

Butter is salted. You can substitute for unsalted butter
and add salt to taste.

It's dangerous to leave hot oil unattended, so make sure
you stay in the kitchen at all times, even while you are
waiting for the oil to heat.